Hawaiian Shirt Designs

Nancy N. Schiffer

77 Lower Valley Road, Atglen, PA 19310

Sincere gratitude is extended to
Howard and Ken
who introduced me to Cindi, to
Cindi
who introduced me to John, and to
John
who opened the treasury.

The team that has shared passions, knowledge, experience, collections,
laughter and time to create this work includes
Howard Auerbach, Rich Breneman, Mark Blackburn, Douglas Congdon-Martin, Roseann Ettinger,
Vernon Kennel, John King, St. Petersburg, Fla., Kenneth Maffia, Larry S. McKaughan, John Miegs,
Dorothy T. Rainwater, Rick and Terri Rasay, Pepe Romero, San Diego, Ca.,
Cindi St. Clair, Peter B. Schiffer, Desire Smith, Dawn Stoltzfus, Kaye and Jim Whitaker (who took the object photos),
Mark Anders, John Tyler Howe, Gregory Ng, Marc Palumbo, Hadley Stern,
and all those who wish to remain anonymous.
Their many contributions are very appreciated.

Library of Congress Cataloging-in-Publication Data

Schiffer, Nancy.
 Hawaiian shirt designs / Nancy N. Schiffer.
  p.   cm.
 Includes bibliographical references and index.
 ISBN 0-7643-0054-7 (hardcover)
 1. Aloha shirts--History. 2. Shirts, Men's--Hawaii. 3. Men's
shirt industry--Hawaii--History. I. Title.
GT617.H3S35   1997
391'.1--dc21   96-37704
                                        CIP
Copyright © 1997 by Schiffer Publishing, Ltd.

Printed in Hong Kong
ISBN: 0-7643-0054-7

Cover Photography by Hadley Stern
Scenic Photography by Douglas Congdon-Martin
Cover & Book Design by Joy Shih Ng

Published by Schiffer Publishing, Ltd.
77 Lower Valley Road
Atglen, PA 19310
Phone: (610) 593-1777
Fax: (610) 593-2002
E-mail: schifferbk@aol.com
Please write for a free catalog.
This book may be purchased from the publisher.
Please include $2.95 for shipping.
Try your bookstore first.

We are interested in hearing from authors
with book ideas on related subjects.

Contents

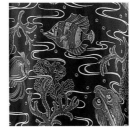
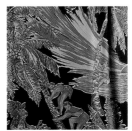

The 'Aloha' Shirt Story

Consider your aloha shirt. Was it designed in Japan, printed in New York, manufactured in Hawaii and sold in Chicago? Perhaps.

But it could have been designed in Hawaii, printed in Japan, manufactured in Honolulu and sold in New York. (Mary Howard Foster, "Hawaiian Style," *Honolulu Star-Bulletin*, April 7, 1956, Magazine Section, p.4.)

The dynamic shirts on the following pages evolved from the special culture of Hawaii — where Asia and the West come together in a paradise of mild climate, clean water, and abundant flowers. The fact that these shirts became enormously popular in the middle of the twentieth century indicates how people responded to the Hawaiian culture, which seemed exotic, romantic, and relaxing. It was the perfect escape.

Through their unusual and often vibrant colors and original fabric designs, aloha shirts and related garments were well suited to the relaxed lifestyle of the local Hawaiian population and provided appealing souvenirs to the increasing numbers of visitors from Asia, Australia, and America. Because they were expensive and 'different' looking from regular sport shirts, and were made with long-lasting fabrics, aloha shirts were considered luxury items that were cherished and not worn out; they were saved as mementos. Their individuality accounts for their preservation and the abundant appreciation they receive today.

Many aloha shirts include phrases from the Hawaiian language in their designs. The 12-letter alphabet of the Hawaiian language was standardized by missionaries in

Label: **Pohaku Made in Hawaii**. Magnificent net fishermen print in ten colors. Rayon. Coconut husk buttons. One perfectly matched pocket.

5

the 1820s. The five vowels (a, e, i, o, and u) and seven consonants (h, k, l, m, n, p, and w) combine phonetically to produce the sonorous words of the Islands.

Before Western contact, native men wore a *malo*, a ten-to-twelve-inch wide strip of *tapa* cloth (made from the inner bark of banana trees), and women wore a *pa-u* skirt, a strip of *tapa* cloth several yards long around the body from the waist. In cool weather they added a *kihei*, rectangular piece of tapa over their shoulders like a cloak. For decoration, they "stamped it [the tapa cloth] with exact and intricate designs." (Buck, vol. V, p. 165.)

Trade with Japan in Hawaiian sandalwood in the early nineteenth century first brought Chinese and Japanese fabrics to the Islands. These imported fabrics began to take the place of tapa cloth for garments. Missionaries taught sewing skills and shared their Western clothing styles so that shirts, trousers, and dresses were normal dress for all by the beginning of the twentieth century.

Palakas

Developing sugar, pineapple, and coffee plantations in the Hawaiian Islands in the first decade of the twentieth century provided jobs for immigrant field workers. Here heavy-duty work shirts of blue and white checked denim known as *palakas* were popular. The Pukui/Elbert *Hawaiian Dictionary* defines "palaka" as "a checkered shirt, usually blue and white, of block print cloth; in the 19th century, a coarse work shirt worn by males, known then in English as a `frock.'" Sailors brought to Hawaii their blue denim trousers known as *sailor mokus*.

Label: **Watumull's and Leilani made in Hawaii.** Blue and white woven plaid fabric. Cotton. Coconut husk buttons.

6

Label: (blue) **Made in Hawaii.** Tailor made from white rice sacks with stitching around the collar. Cotton. White porcelain buttons.

During the early twentieth century, many women produced clothing for their families in their homes. Custom tailor shops in plantation towns and Honolulu, most of them owned by Asians, supplied the local market with more formal clothing. Shirts with short sleeves were made for day wear, while long sleeves were warmer and made for formal night wear. The following advertisement, typical of its time, was placed by a "shirtmaker" whose wife was a "dressmaker." (*Husted's Directory of Honolulu*, 1903, p. 603.)

Label: None. Light brown with Asian mark stamps in black and brown against a background of dotted squares. Silk. Coconut shell buttons. Long sleeves.

Pioneer Shirt Factory of Honolulu. No. 17 Emma Street. The undersigned begs to inform the public of these islands that he is making Shirts by measurement. Directions for self-measurement will be given on application. White shirts, over shirts, and night gowns. A fit guaranteed by making a sample shirt to every order. Island orders solicited. A. M. Mellis. ("History From Our Files. Sixty Years Ago—1889." *Honolulu Advertiser*, May 9, 1949, Ed. p., c.4.)

Dry goods stores in Honolulu advertised yard-goods and ready-made clothing imported from American and foreign sources, such as this advertisement from The Liberty House:

Women's Wear of Distinction. New York and Paris Modes Transposed to Meet Hawaii's Needs. Something New by Every Steamer. Write for Samples of Pima Cloth and Pongee. *Paradise of the Pacific*, March, 1920, p. 7)

Hawaiian Clothing Factories Begin

A new venture in Hawaii was first advertised in 1922 as follows:

Hawaii Clothing Mfg. Co., Ltd. Manufacturers of Men's, Ladies' and Children's Wearing Apparel. The Pioneer Clothing Manufacturing House in the Hawaiian Islands. Be sure your garment has our trade-mark. Wholesale Only. Kuwili Street, Near Pine, Honolulu, T. H. (*Polk-Husted Directory Company's Directory of Honolulu and the Territory of Hawaii* for 1922, page 355.)

Label: **Musa-shiya Shoten the Shirtmaker also kimono make dry good sell 179 N. King St. Honolulu.** This label corresponds to early advertisements in the address and to advertisements in so far as it contains the pidgin phrase 'also kimono make dry good sell' (see *All About Hawaii*, 1954, p. 35). Brown Japanese lanterns on a gray and white triangles background. Rayon crepe. Coconut husk buttons. c. 1928.

Musa-Shiya The Shirtmaker

During the 1920s, dry goods stores continued to supply fabrics for home sewing, and one eventually began making shirts itself by accident.

The real pioneers in business had a language barrier to crash, which sent many back to their homelands thoroughly discouraged.

Chotaro Miyamoto came from Japan in 1890, and started a little dry goods business. When his American-born son, Koichiro, was six years old, he was sent according to Japanesse custom, back to Japan to go to school.

When Chotaro died, in 1915, the young Koichiro came back to take over his father's business. He spoke practically no English, nor did he have much knowledge of American ways.

Shipping was uncertain, and the young man impatient. When orders didn't come, he ordered again. Now as sometimes happens with overseas shipments, came a day when several back orders arrived at one time. There was young Miyamoto, suddenly surrounded with bolt upon bolt of the finest English broadcloth. The store overflowed and more was on the dock.

Now fine broadcloth in those days meant only one thing. Fine Shirts. So the young merchant sought out the finest seamstresses in Honolulu, and they began making fine shirts indeed. Koichiro sought the advice of an advertising specialist, George Mellen, who saw in the merchant's bumbling pidgin English the makings of a series of ads. (*Honolulu Advertiser*, June 23, 1959, Sec. XI, p.12.)

9

This ad was accompanied by a trade mark of the company's initials. Hawaii Clothing Mfg. Co. continued to be listed in the directories until 1930. In 1932, the company's name was changed to Sailor Moku Products, Ltd.

Also in March of 1922, the Union Supply Company was founded, primarily to manufacture plantation uniforms including denim work pants, overalls, shoes, suitcases and trunks. The company was listed between 1928 and 1964 as a clothing manufacturer. "Its products are distributed throughout the territory and the company also supplies the Army and Navy with garments." (*Honolulu Star-Bulletin*, May 2, 1932, p.3.)

The organization of these companies marks the first clothing factories in Hawaii, and both of them were begun to supply work clothes to the plantations. From that start, an industry grew that would employ thousands of people and help stimulate the Hawaiian economy.

And so Musa-Shiya The Shirtmaker was in a new business, using Fuji silk and other fabrics besides his broadcloth. (*Ibid.*) He ran a series of amusing newspaper ads to promote his shirts, and from them we can learn about the development of his business. An example follows:

OH HAPPY SPRINGTIME. Here arrive Springs on gentle foot but hardly can tell from Winter going which have gentle movement in Hawaii also. But feeling difference inside. Feeling very glad to do something but not work. Feeling kinely feeling for sweetheart also. Funny kine weather. Here are neatural consequence NEW SPRING SHIRT. (*Ibid.*)

Musa-Shiya featured a Happi coat in an ad of about 1926. (*Ibid.*)

There were many other custom tailors in Honolulu with similar businesses, but they were not advertising as much or as well as Musa-Shiya; therefore, details about their work are not able to be known.

Tourism is Growing

During the 1920s, an increasing number of wealthy travelers came to Hawaii for vacation, some came for military duty, and all took a first look at this exotic place. To accommodate them, new hotels were built, including the magnificent Royal Hawaiian Hotel on Waikiki Beach. Nearby were the surfing beaches and Diamond Head Point which drew the travelers to their natural beauty.

The Thirties

The Chamber of Commerce of Honolulu organized the first Hawaiian Products Week to promote locally manufactured products. Enormously successful, it prompted future annual Weeks and gave local people pride in their products. The Chamber also worked to draw attention, through the press, the movies, and the business community, to the uniqueness of Hawaii. The following Hollywood-made movies about Hawaii expanded the appeal of the islands when they were released in the United States in the 1930s:

1932 *Bird of Paradise* with Delores Del Rio
1934 *Nearby Hawaii*
1937 *Waikiki Wedding* with Bing Crosby and Martha Raye
1938 *Hawaii Calls*
1939 *Hawaiian Nights*
1939 *Honolulu*

In 1932, the same Chamber of Commerce prepared a report which claimed that

Palakas and sailor-mokus have grown to be almost a national costume— so typically Hawaiian are they. The grass skirt that strangers visualize on dusky maids is seldom seen, but palakas— blue and white checked denim shirts— and sailor mokus— blue denim trousers—have their places in the wardrobes of every islander. For years the laborer has worn a palaka to work; it has been a part of the cowboy's picturesque costume; and stevedores have worn them on the docks. In recent years the smart set of Hawaii have annexed the palaka and sailor mokus to their wardrobes. Boys and girls wear them to school, to play, to foot-ball games, to parties; the younger set wear them to house parties, to cocktail parties and beach parties; and one of Hawaii's most charming matron, going to the mountains on her honeymoon, wore a palaka with riding breeches and boots as a going-away costume at her wedding. *Industries in Hawaii*, 1932.)

The shirts were gradually taking a place in the society.
In 1933, Musa-Shiya The Shirtmaker's newspaper advertisements were compiled into a booklet, as advertised in the *Honolulu Star-Bulletin*, April 21, p. 5:

> Note: To meet the demand for examples of the shirt-maker's adventures in advertising a collection has been published in a booklet 'How Musa-Shiya the Shirtmaker Broke into Print.' Price 25 cents at book stores or publisher, 410 Kauikeolani Building.

In 1934, one of his advertisements included a welcome to President Franklin Roosevelt and his family to Hawaii.

> Musa-Shiya The Shirtmaker (also kimono makes and pajama makes). My only one shop 1915 S. King Streets nearly corner Alakea Streets. Kangei! Hon. President Roosevelt!...I am hoping your favorable health and eternally. *Honolulu Star-Bulletin* Roosevelt [visit] Edition, first section, July 26, 1934, p.5.)

The Roosevelts' visit, in July of 1934, added significantly to the image of Hawaii as a respectable and interesting destination for Americans and Asians alike.

Label: **Musa-shiya the Shirtmaker Waikiki, Honolulu** (with the countenance of the Shirtmaker himself). Unidentified birds on a lavender background. Rayon crepe. Oyster shell buttons. Long sleeves. c. 1935.

Label: None. Tailor made. This shirt is a typical example of the early Japanese style shirt. The print includes cranes, samurai helmets, and other Japanese elements against a background of gold and dark brown. Eight colors on white silk. Coconut husk buttons. Two flapped pockets and long sleeves. c. mid-1930s.

The Fabrics

The yardgoods most frequently available in Hawaii in the early 1930s included Japanese silk prints, raw silk material, batik, cotton yukata or kimono cloth, and rayon from the United States Mainland.

Silk

Asian clothing styles were prevalent in Honolulu, and after 1900 shirts of "gaily colored Japanese silk" were custom made in increasing numbers by Asian tailors. The same fabrics were used for children's clothing in Japan and adult sportswear in the islands. (Brown, pp.106-108).

Rayon

Rayon was first produced in 1884 through the nitro cellulose method by a French chemist, Count de Chardonnet. It was known as artificial silk. The name "rayon" was adopted by the trade in 1924 and the Viscose Co. alone produced 28,000,000 pounds that year. In 1928 the Rayon Institute of America, Inc. was organized by a group of rayon producers to conduct a national campaign of education. In that same year rayon received the widespread commendation of the most famous Parisian couturiers, as well as the foremost American stylists and designers (see The Story of Rayon, Second Edition, 1929, The Viscose Company, pp. 7-19.)

Batik

     In 1935, batik from Java became a popular yardgood, judging from the frequency of their appearance in ads. Watumull's East India Store advertised "New Shipment of Java Batiks, Colorful Prints, Handmade in All Color Combinations. The Latest Fad in Bathing Suits, Trunks and Bandannas for Beach Wear. A Large Variety of Sizes." (*Honolulu Advertiser*, May 19, 1935, p.2.) Their popularity in Hawaii may have stimulated the development of Hawaiian designs for textiles.

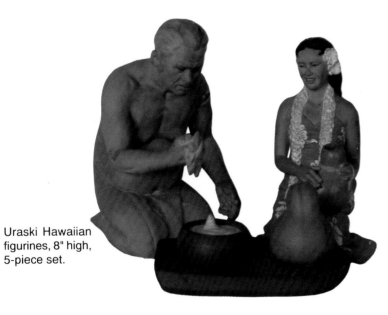

Uraski Hawaiian figurines, 8" high, 5-piece set.

13

Label: **The Store for Men Marshall Field & Company Sports Apparel Made in Honolulu.** Yellow and black terry cloth print. Cotton. Coconut buttons. Two waist patch pockets. c.1940.

Hawaiian Fabric Designs Begin

Gump's department store in Honolulu placed the first newspaper advertisement mentioning specifically Hawaiian fabric designs on July 7, 1935, in the *Honolulu Advertiser*, p. 12:

Fabrics Depicting Hawaiian Floral Designs.
Made Exclusively for Gump's Opposite Royal
Hawaiian Hotel.

Therefore, Hawaiian prints were apparently available in Hawaii in 1935. Watumull's East India Store took a leading role in the promotion of Hawaiian fabric designs. In 1936, Mr. G. J. Watumull, owner of the East India store, commissioned his sister-in-law, artist Elsie Das, to produce fifteen floral designs for Hawaiian fabric prints. She painted her designs onto fabric, and samples were sent to Japan to be hand blocked onto raw silk. (William Davenport, "Elsie Das, Artist-Designer," *Paradise of the Pacific*, vol. 65, no. 9, September, 1963, p. 18.)

These subtle floral patterns modern and dynamic in concept, were the first Hawaiian designs to be produced commercially. Beautifully executed, they were a huge commercial success and achieved the added distinction of being bought by a number of schools and colleges for inclusion in their textile collections. They sold by the boat load and were exhibited as far away as London.

14

Label: None. Anonymous tailor made. Grey and white caladiums on yellow background. Rayon. Oyster shell buttons, two patch pockets, size tag sewn into collar. c. 1935.

Elsie Das continued to produce original Hawaiian designs up to the Second World War. Once, she recalls, through an error on the part of Japanese manufacturers, a group of her designs were printed on heavy satin. These started a vogue in Hollywood. Ginger Rogers, Janet Gaynor and other stars bought bolts of the stuff and had it made up into 'seductive gowns.' The result was an epidemic of Hawaiian designs, with hibiscus and ginger breaking out on table cloths, napkins and scarves all over the country.

Meanwhile Elsie's original designs were being reproduced in *Studio Year Book*, *House and Garden*, *The Christian Science Monitor* and other national publications. And the artist herself without suspecting it, was revolutionizing summer styles by doing designs on lightweight rayon fabric which, in the middle thirties, were made up into Aloha shirts. These became the rage. Hawaiian designs were printed in New York and the Aloha shirt was here to stay. *(Ibid.)*

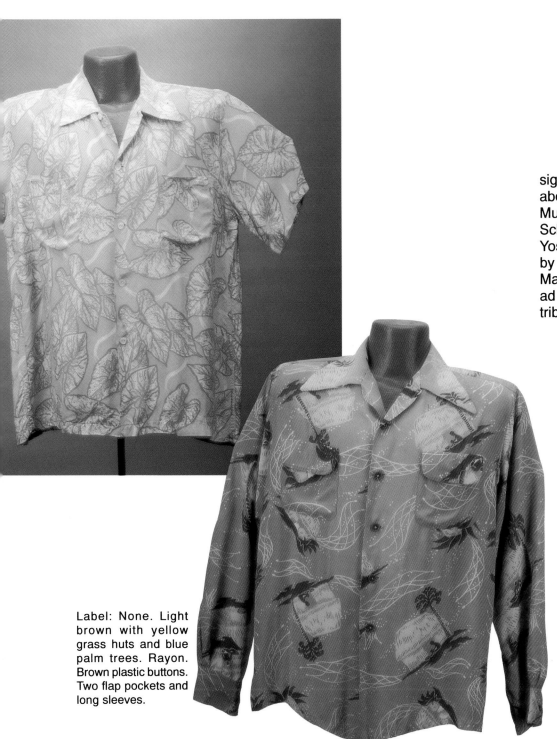

Label: None. Light brown with yellow grass huts and blue palm trees. Rayon. Brown plastic buttons. Two flap pockets and long sleeves.

Other designers were also producing Hawaiian designs, such as Nobuji Yoshida who had come to Hawaii about 1918 from Yamaguchi, Japan. He had studied at the Museum School of Fine Arts in Boston and at the Blockerer Schule in Munich. (Annabel Damon, "Elsie Das, Nobuji Yoshida Pioneers in Island Designs," from data compiled by John MacMillan, *Honolulu Advertiser*, Woman's World, March 24, 1950, p.4.) Also, Hawaiian artist Isami Doi and ad designer Jerry Chong of the *Honolulu Advertiser* contributed designs for early Hawaiian prints. (*Ibid.*)

Coconut Buttons

In the June 18, 1935 issue of the *Honolulu Advertiser*, p. 4, an advertisement for Eastman Kodak Stores includes coconut buttons:

> For Summer Dresses, Coconut Buttons. Smartest Vogue of the Year! Artistically designed in 100 Original Hawaiian Motifs. Beautifully Carved from Coconut Shell and Highly Polished. Many Sizes. Get them while they are in a large variety very reasonably priced. Eastman Kodak Stores, 1059 Fort St. and on the Beach at Waikiki—2041 Kalakaua Ave.

It appears that by June of 1935, the ingredients for the aloha shirts as we now know them were in place in Hawaii. So who put it all together?

Label: **Musa-shiya the Shirtmaker Honolulu, Hawaii** (with the countenance of the Shirtmaker himself). Brown tropical design with palm trees, hulas girls, and surfers. Note the line of stitching around the collar and the "darts" near the sleeves. Silk. Brown plastic buttons. c. 1940.

Label: None. Anonymous tailor made. Green, yellow and tan palm trees, hula girls, and surfers on blue background. Rayon. Plastic buttons. Frayed size tag sewn into collar. c. 1935.

'Aloha' Shirts First Advertised

Musa-Shiya The Shirtmaker was both enthusiastic and business smart. He placed the first advertisement using the term "Aloha shirts" in 1935 in the *Honolulu-Advertiser* on June 28, p. 17:

Honolulu's Noted Shirt Maker and Kimono Shop. 'Aloha' shirts — well tailored, beautiful designs and radiant colors. Ready-made or made to order...95 cents up.

Musa-Shiya repeated this wording in ads during July, 1935; and in July of 1936 he included his address at 179 N. King Street and his phone number. (*Honolulu Advertiser*, in 1935, July 5, p.9; July 12, p.14; July 18, p.9; and July 26, p.9; and in 1936, July 2, p.3 and July 10, p.9.)

The use of the term *aloha* here for sport shirts made in Hawaii therefore dates from June of 1935. The term itself may have grown from local street talk, since the shirts were being made in the early 1930s from Asian prints.

In 1935 and 1936, as the tourist trade and the frequency of visits by vessels of the United States Navy increased, there were growing demands for Hawaiian souvenirs. The word 'aloha' was used in connection with numerous advertisements, products and business firms. In 1935 and 1936 when the word 'Aloha' was attached to many types of merchandise, it was not unique that it also was attached to shirts and sportswear. (Fundaburk, vol. ii, p. 43.)

But another explanation of the 'first' advertising with the term 'Aloha' is made by Harriet Ray, an advertising salesman for the *Honolulu Advertiser*, who stated,

...it was born in 1935 and that she and merchandiser Ellery Chun named it. "Ellery and I ran the very first aloha shirt ad in *The Advertiser*. Our own Jerry Chong (now *Advertiser* art director) did the sketch. The ad showed shirt-tails out and tied in a bow — as a fashion tip. Stuck for a name, we hastily dubbed it `the Aloha Shirt.'" ("New Look in Shirts," *Honolulu Star Bulletin and Advertiser*, Aloha, May 20, 1962, pp. 6-7.)

Label: **Ka-lae Hawaii.**
Dark blue with white sailor design, a shore leave fantasy gone haywire - the hunter becomes the hunted. Cotton. Blue porcelain buttons. c. 1939.

18

Hawaiian fabric yardage.
Rayon. c. 1940s.

'Aloha' Trademark and Label Registered

Ellery Chun owned the King-Smith dry goods store at 36 N. King Street near Smith until 1950. In 1936, "many local boys were wearing `Aloha' type shirts made of Japanese challis and local Filipinos were wearing a bright shirt-tail-out shirt called a `bayau' or `friend,' because they liked the shirt... " (Fundaburk, vol. 4, p. 169, footnote 1.)

Cloth left over from Oriental kimonos was probably fashioned into bright colored shirts which school boys wore on special festive days. As more young people wore the shirts for casual occasions, the tourists saw them and requested to have them made. Mr. Chun stated that his father had a ready-to-wear shop where he began to work as a young man. As he saw the beach boys directing customers to a tailor shop next door, to have bright colored shirts made from Oriental prints, he conceived the idea that if such shirts were made up in anticipation of customer demands[,] this might appeal to the tourists, because there would be a waiting period for tailoring. (Fundaburk, vol. 2, p. 393, footnote 77.)

Mr. Chun took action on his idea, and formally registered a trade mark for Aloha sportswear on July 15, 1936. The mark had a sketch of a bending palm tree and the lettering

Styled in Hawaii
Aloha
Sportswear
Made in Hawaii

The registration covered the trademark's use for twenty years on "such goods or manufactured articles being described as follows: Wearing apparel, including shirts, cravats, slacks, bathing suits and trunks, trousers, underwear, and merchandise of such nature... [and] used on labels, postcards, letterheads, wrappers, signs, and all advertising matters to promote sales." The label was separately registered on October 26, 1937 for a period of twenty years, "such LABEL to be applied directly to men's, women's and children's shirts of every description, color and design." (Fundaburk, vol. 2, p. 67 and 68.)

Shirt Factories Begin

Two companies were founded in 1936, in Honolulu, to produce shirts in large quantities in factories, and to distribute them to a wider market. These were Branfleet Sportswear Company and Kamehameha Garment Company.

George Brangier and Nathaniel Norfleet had experience in the wholesale and retail clothing markets before they formed Branfleet Sportswear Company in January of 1936. They began by contracting with Wong's Products of Honolulu to produce shirts, and they set about developing the distribution and marketing for them. Before too long they set up their own production plant at North King Street. ("New Branfleet Sports Wear Factory Opens," *Honolulu Advertiser*, July 23, 1939, p.6.)

Herbert Briner founded Kamehameha Garment Company, also in 1936. Kamehameha produced sportswear, including shirts, at 800-B South Beretania Street and established some of the first overseas sales accounts for Hawaiian clothing.

Branfleet and Kamehameha thus changed the production of the majority of Hawaiian-made sport shirts from a tailor-made to a factory-made business.

By October of 1936, there were eleven clothing manufacturers and fifteen shirt manufacturers listed in a business directory put out by the Chamber of Commerce of Honolulu.

Max Lewis founded the Royal Hawaiian Manufacturing Co. in 1937. Within a decade it became owned by Watumull stores to supply their sportswear. Opportunity seemed to be in the calm, fragrant air.

King-Smith store advertisements in the late 1930s included the trade name 'Aloha.' In November of 1939, this ad appeared:

Men's and ladies' cotton 'Aloha' Shirts 1.00 each. Well known King-Smith originations in name and tailoring, in either button front or pullover style and a variety of attractive patterns and colors. Buy several at the Factory Surplus Sale Price! Sizes XS, S, M, L.

Men's and women's — silk 'Aloha' Shirts 1.95. Our regular quality regularly priced much more. Good wearing silk material King-Smith fashioned in In-or-Outer style with genuine coconut buttons. Sizes XS, S, M, L, XL.

Boys 'Aloha' Play Suits (As illustrated). Shorts now 95 cents. Shirts now 95 cents. Smart little play suits, made of Pineapple cloth with Hawaiian emblem. Good Wearing. Washable. Colors Natural, Blue, Maize, Brown, Navy, Boy Blue stripes. Sizes 2 to 14.

Creators of 'Aloha' shirts and 'Waikiki' fashions. (*Honolulu Advertiser*, November 5, 1939, Society Section, p. 3. and *Honolulu Star-Bulletin*, November 2, 1939, p. 13.)

The shirt of 'pineapple cloth' in the illustration also has the 'Hawaiian emblem' as indicated in the King-Smith ad.

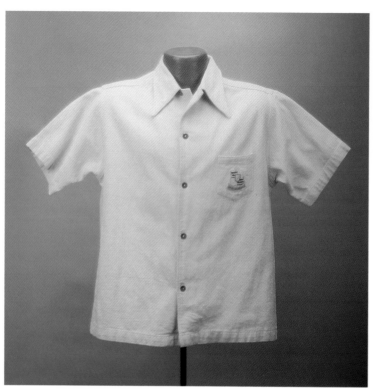

The Pineapple Tweed. Label: **Designed by Duke Kahanamoku World Champion Swimmer made in The Hawaiian Islands.** The so called "pineapple tweed" cloth is solid yellow peppered with tiny imperfections in the yarn (reminiscent of homespun) and is double stitched. An embroidered Royal Hawaiian Crest is sewn on the patch pocket. The collar buttons to a button hole. The collar points are long, diagonal, and flared with stitching along the edge. The material is very heavy and coarse cotton with a noticeable slub. Small flat coconut shell buttons. c. 1940. Cloth and shirt probably made by Branfleet Sportswear in Honolulu.

Label: **Pony Express Fisch Trade Mark Reg. Pat. Pend. Made in California** (separately) **Andrade Honolulu Sportswear** (separately) **Hand wash use cool iron.** Tan gabardine with saddle stitched collar. Cotton. Domed plastic buttons. Two flap saddle bag pockets. c. 1935. The crest is contemporary, the embroidery recent.

Branfleet made the Kahala and Duke Kahanamoku beachwear which was advertised by the King-Smith store as "The '39 Duke Kahanamoku Ocean Wear" and "Duke Kahanamoku" swim suits.

[The] Most popular product of this house is the ever-popular Duke Kahanamoku jacket, for men and women. A new version of the famous Duke jacket is about to appear, but until it does the exact details are a secret with Branfleet.

Cottons and kala cloth from the Mainland are the fabrics most frequently used by this manufacturing house. Kala cloth, a new fabric, was made for Branfleet from a combination of cotton, wool and rayon after extensive experimentation. This material is washable and is perfect for life in Hawaii or playtime anywhere.

Exclusive fabric patterns of this house include the lovely hula pattern which depicts the feather gourds and rattle of sticks by beautiful dancers at the court of King Kalakaua.

Other patterns are the crown flower, in which nature takes her design from a Queen's coronet; the pattern royal, in which are woven the royal feather capes of the old alii; the aloha pattern, a carefree melange of Island subjects such as the Aloha tower and scarlet hibiscus leis. (Lorna Arlen, *Ibid.*)

Later, in 1951, the company was renamed Kahala Sportswear, Ltd.

Label: **Duke Champion Kahanamoku Ho'omanau Nui (Take It Easy) Jacket.** (Very unusual label.) Multi-color border print with yellow background and scene of Diamond Head viewed from inside a grove of graceful coconut palms. Rayon. Oyster shell buttons, two patch pockets. c. 1940.

21

By 1939, Kamehameha was exporting sportswear to the United States Mainland, Canada, England, Australia and New Zealand. (Lorna Arlen, "Pins and Needles in Hawaii," *Honolulu Advertiser*, February 19, 1939, Magazine Section, p.1.) The cotton cloth was printed in the U.S. Mainland and by 1939 included "approximately 100 styles in this line and there are 23 exclusive print patterns. One of the newest of these is a diary' print, with such phrases as the following written over it in a feminine script, `Last night on the beach...Tomorrow I leave...fun at the Royal...' Novelty shorts in topsail cloth, to be worn with aloha shirts, are another of this manufacturer's smartest new styles." (*Ibid.*)

> The well-known insignia of Kamehameha, with the Hawaiian motto meaning, 'The life of the land is perpetuated in righteousness' is owned by Branfleet and is used on the Duke jackets and shirts and is incorporated in an attractive 'Ka Moi' fabric pattern...(Lorna Arlen, *Ibid.*)

In 1939, Nat Norfleet, of Branfleet, made amusing comments in an interview about how sportswear from Hawaii was viewed by foreign buyers:

> Even the buyers of the biggest stores think that Hawaiian sportswear is made by natives in grass huts on the beach. We even heard that one Mainland business man thought that the dyes in the prints were stamped into the fabric by native women with their feet! They have other weird notions about their being

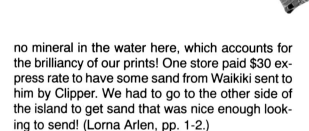

no mineral in the water here, which accounts for the brilliancy of our prints! One store paid $30 express rate to have some sand from Waikiki sent to him by Clipper. We had to go to the other side of the island to get sand that was nice enough looking to send! (Lorna Arlen, pp. 1-2.)

We see that the shirt business that developed in Hawaii in the 1930s opened international markets and turned the attention of the fashion world toward Hawaii for the first time.

> The aloha shirt—symbol of the comfortable, gay and picturesque sportswear that is made and designed in Hawaii—has become Big Business. (Lorna Arlen, "Pins and Needles in Hawaii," *Honolulu Advertiser*, Magazine Section, February 19, 1939.)

Label: (green) **Kamehameha made and styled in Hawaii.** Green background with white lettering "pa'i kapa" and scenes of people and feather capes. Rayon. Coconut shell buttons. c. 1940s. Special shirt. The fabric was probably designed by Kahala (Branfleet).

Label: **Watumull's Honolulu Made in Hawaii.** White eagles and yellow pine trees on dark blue background. Rayon crepe, coconut shell buttons. c. 1940.

Label: **Watumull's Honolulu Made in Hawaii.** Note the **dry clean only** tag. Brown eagles and yellow pine trees on dark blue background. Rayon crepe, coconut shell buttons. c. 1940.

The Forties

Increasing activities of the U.S. Fleet in the Pacific area in the early 1940s brought sailors and increasing private travel companies brought more civilians to Hawaii. The presence of travelers stimulated the production of goods with Hawaiian motifs. Hollywood studios continued to make movies in the early 1940s about romantic Hawaiian life. Some of the popular ones were:

1941 *Aloma of the South Seas*
1941 *Abbott and Costello in the Navy*
1942 *Song of the Islands* with Betty Grable
      and Victor Mature
1943 *White Savage* with Jon Hall,
      Maria Montez, and Sabu

Cruise ships of the Matson Navigation Company of San Francisco and other cruise ship lines promoted luxury travel to Hawaii for wealthy passengers. For daily menus during these cruises, the Matson Line commissioned artists to make Hawaiian theme images that would put their passengers in a casual Hawaiian frame of mind while they were crossing the ocean. American artist Frank MacIntosh painted for them strong images of native girls with leis and romantic sunsets that were used on menus for Matson Line's S.S. *Lurline* and S. S. *Matsonia* in 1939, 1940, and 1941. Later, some of these images were adapted to designs for fabrics that were made into aloha shirts.

Label: **The Liberty House Honolulu Waikiki.** Print derived from Frank Macintosh menu cover design in multi-colors and letters H and A made from flowers on gray background. Rayon crepe. Coconut shell buttons, matching pocket. c. 1950.

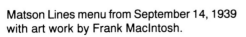

Matson Lines menu from September 14, 1939
with art work by Frank MacIntosh.

Label: **Young Aloha Honolulu.** Dark green with
Hawaiian figures after an original design by Frank
MacIntosh. Rayon. Green plastic buttons. c. 1950.

25

A gradual change was taking place at this time in Hawaiian fabric printing.

The newest development here is the use of hand-blocked designs on monotone fabrics. A new process has been developed whereby the dye is made absolutely waterfast. This use of a monotone fabric, with a subtle hand-blocked Polynesian motif, is being accepted eagerly by those to whom the riotous Hawaiian prints are no longer a novelty...(*Pan Pacific*, Vol. 4, No. 1, January-March, 1940, pp.77-79.)

By 1941, Hawaiian artists were increasingly using these block printing methods in small shops in Honolulu to put their original designs on fabrics. Many of the pattern ideas at this time came from artifacts at the Bishop Museum of anthropology in Honolulu which has a large collection of original tapa cloths. "Our original patterns were very beautiful, and it is regrettable that from that beginning developed all the corn." (Leo Israel, as quoted by Ligaya Fruto, "Getting Away from Corny," *Honolulu Star-Bulletin*, December 15, 1964, Sec. C, p. 3.)

2 6

Label: **Lehua Hilo, Hawaii.** Light brown with scattered drum, helmet, and leaf pattern on crackled background. Silk. Molded plastic buttons with Asian writing.

Hawaiian Design Comes Into Its Own

War came to Hawaii at Pearl Harbor near Honolulu on December 7, 1942. The place has never been quite the same. During the next three years, the production of aloha shirts in Hawaii came into its own. Shirt production was expanded because the scarcity of men's shirts from the U.S. Mainland and Asian sources made them needed by local residents, and they were seen as appropriate souvenirs by the increased number of service personnel. "Through block printing, the hula girl or *Aloha Oe* could be conspicuously superimposed on wearing apparel. It made good gifts, souvenirs, and was like a postcard that could be worn." (John Brosnan, "Men and Money at Work," *Honolulu Star-Bulletin*, January 31, 1953, Feature Section, p.1.) While commercially isolated, Hawaiian shirt manufacturers relied on local retailers for sales and Honolulu residents became more accustomed to purchasing Hawaiian-made garments. Their habits were not much altered when the war ended in the Pacific area in August of 1945.

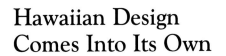

Label: None. Purple with pink flowers labeled "Lehua." Rayon. Coconut husk buttons. 1940s.

In 1945 and 1946, government restrictions on price ceilings influenced manufacturers to make men's sport shirts - not dress shirts, bathing trunks - not boxer shorts, and women's suits - not men's suits; so men's clothing was scarce in the market place. Clothing produced in Hawaii continued to sell in Hawaii, while Mainland goods gradually arrived in ever-larger quantities. But so, too, did exports to the Mainland gradually grow. Filene's department store in Boston and Lord & Taylor in New York ran successful Hawaiian promotions in the post-war era, aided by the cruise lines and Pan American Airways, and the Hawaii Visitors Bureau.

To meet the greater demand for shirts and other clothing, more fabrics were needed in an increasing number of designs. "The small local manufacturer couldn't produce enough yardage. When it came to real yardage, they couldn't do it. So big Mainland firms had to take over." (Ligaya Fruto, *Honolulu Star-Bulletin*, December 15, 1964, Sec. C, p. 3.) Roller printing methods at New York manufacturing plants produced the required quantities at competitive prices.

The status of the shirt market in Hawaii in 1946 was described from one writer's point of view in the following article:

Hula dancer nodding figures, 1940s, 6 1/2" high.

Next time you ask a bosom friend for the shirt off his back specify aloha shirt (it's a better deal).

Aloha shirts are a $60,000 a month business in Hawaii and could be twice that if there were enough material available for making more of these colorful representations of the islands...

The Samoan tapa patterns were one of the first to be used in aloha shirts when the initial ones were made a little more than 10 years ago. They still lead the field in popularity.

Aloha shirt makers (there are several of them in Honolulu) have about 60 different patterns in stock — patterns that they bring back from time to time.

Yearly the larger garment firms here have their artists design from 10 to 15 new patterns. The designs are sent to the Mainland where they are printed on French crepe, shantung, cotton, spun rayon or almost any material that is available.

The colored patterns, usually red, blue, yellow, aqua, white and tan, are sent to Hawaii to be manufactured into shirts.

Men usually buy shirts with figures on them while women seem to prefer those with floral designs.

Current favorite designs are tapa, fish net, holoku, island map, bamboo, hukilau, song of the islands and other ideas.

The bolts of aloha shirt cloth are cut into 10 pieces and are sewed into shirts within two to three weeks after their arrival from the Mainland.

The aloha shirt, an exclusive island idea and product is seldom seen on the Mainland. Bing Crosby, for years, has been its chief proponent, and Bing is said to have brought this bit of Hawaii to the Mainland after his first visit to the Territory. (Harry Lambeth, "Aloha Shirts Add Local Color," *Honolulu Star-Bulletin*, October 31, 1946, p. 13.)

Labels: **An Original Hand Painted Garment by Kealoha of Hawaii** (separately) **Nani of Hawaii Honolulu.** Cream colored background with painted calabash and pink lei on the front right side and kneeling lady with pink lei and mountain scene on the back. Rayon. Long sleeves and coconut shell buttons. This is very unusual with carefully controlled silk screen painting in a particularly lovely design. c. 1950.

30

Label: **Royal Hawaiian Made and styled in Hawaii.** Brown tapa design. Cotton. Coconut husk buttons. c. 1951.

Label: **Kamehameha made and styled in Hawaii.** Yellow with black and red bamboo design. Nylon. Coconut husk buttons. c.1950.

Honolulu Men's Summer Attire Studied

In 1946 and for the previous twenty years, professional men in Hawaii had considered adopting more comfortable clothes than the coat and tie on hot days. In the mid-nineteen forties, air conditioning was not typical, but trade winds were used for cooling offices and homes. On a few occasions, groups took action to address this problem. One was the business community in Honolulu.

The Honolulu Chamber of Commerce, collectively sweltering over a hot desk during the warm Hawaiian summer, has decided to do something about men's clothes.

The Chamber president announced Wednesday that $1,000 has been appropriated so a committee can seriously study and prepare suitable designs for businessmen's clothing, 'with the view of making them more comfortable and practical.'...

First of all, is the gaily colored aloha shirt or the plain white T-shirt to be standard attire for trust company executives? ("Chamber Decides to do Something About Men's Garb," *Honolulu Advertiser*, September 26, 1946, p. 2.)

With prodding from the Chamber of Commerce, in August of 1947, the Board of Supervisors of the City and County of Honolulu passed a resolution favoring the wearing of sport shirts by City and County employees from June 1 to October 31 each year. This act has had far reaching effect beyond the borders of Hawaii, as many businesses in

Embossed ceramic souvenir plate, 1950s.

the rest of the world gradually have adopted more casual clothing styles in hot weather. And this trend was very good for the growing popularity of aloha shirts.

Aloha Weeks

The advent of Aloha Week in 1947, the successor to Hawaiian Products Weeks of the 1930s, successfully focused attention on aloha shirts as appropriate attire at the week's activities. By the 1948 Aloha Week, men and women in the community made a dynamic effort to cooperate with the organizers by wearing Hawaiian garments and advertising local products. This special week has since grown into a local event of huge proportions right up to the present.

Label: (black) **Made in Hawaii.** Red with white silk screened surfers design on the right shoulder. Rayon with a linen-like texture. Red plastic buttons. c. 1950.

Old Prints Renewed

Along with the growing popularity of aloha shirts themselves, fabric designers also were busy and successful in adapting old and creating new designs. In the late 1940s, many copies of tapa cloth designs and Elsie Das' and other designers' work from ten years earlier were prevalent.

Screen Printing in Honolulu

As a young man working in his family's custom tailoring business in Honolulu, Alfred Shaheen became frustrated with the long wait for fabric from the Mainland. In 1947, Alfred Shaheen began a screen printing factory in Honolulu to supply reprints of popular patterns very quickly. His business grew in size and developed new techniques into the 1950s.

Label: **Penney's Topflight Hand Washable Rayon.** Green with white shaded bars and orange spirals design. White plastic buttons. Two patch pockets. c. 1950.

Matson Line Resumes Cruises

The Matson line's ships *Lurline* and *Matsonia* had been converted to troop carriers during the war, but in April of 1948, the *Lurline* was officially decommissioned and sailed again with private travelers to Hawaii. Two designs for aloha shirts are connected with these events.

The menu covers for dinners on Matson cruises again featured artists' romanticized views of Hawaiian scenes. Back in 1938 to 1940, Matson had commissioned American artist Eugene Savage to paint six four-by-eight-foot murals depicting Hawaiian\Polynesian traditions and history. When the murals were finished, the ships were already involved in the war effort, so the murals were stored. But on the first voyage of the post-war era, Savage's designs made their debut on the menus and were immediately popular beyond belief. By 1952, 250,000 menu covers [of six different designs] had been distributed. ("Matson Menu Covers that Became Hawaiian Classics," c. 1965.) These menus were in use on Matson cruises at least until 1957.

The adaptation of Savage's mural designs from menus to fabrics was completed in the late 1940s when shirts and women's sportswear were made with the "Island Feast" design by Kamehameha. These are prize finds today.

Label: (green) **Kamehameha made and styled in Hawaii.** Selvage printed: **"Original Matson Menu Design" by Eugene Savage.** Multi-colored scenic print design derived from the mural "Island Feast" by Eugene Savage. Rayon. c. 1950.

Fabric designs showing the cruise ship *Lurline* also were made into aloha shirts, probably in the first few years of the 1950s. They are shown with the text about 1950s shirts.

Custom designers from Honolulu produced Hawaii's first high style lines of women's clothing for travel conscious cruise customers. Aloha shirts were not just for the beach anymore.

The fabric and clothing manufacturers, who began to recognize their common problems and think of themselves as parts of an industry, formed the Hawaii Garment Manufacturers Guild in 1949 and established programs over the next decade to promote their businesses. Fortunately, Hawaiian print clothing continued to grow in popularity to support their efforts.

Label: (green) **Kamehameha made and styled in Hawaii.** Selvage printed: **"Original Matson Menu Design" by Eugene Savage.** Multi-colored scenic print design derived from the mural "Island Feast" by Eugene Savage. Rayon. Coconut husk buttons, long sleeves. A magnificent design beautifully printed and shown to advantage in this long-sleeved shirt. c. 1950.

35

Matson Lines menu dated 1956 with cover print of a mural design from 1938-1940 entitled *Island Feast* by Eugene Savage.

The Fifties

Let's Dress Hawaiian

The volume and popularity of aloha shirts was spectacular in the 1950s, due in no small part to the efforts of movie makers from California. Among the popular films with top stars were:

1950 *Pagan Love Song* with Esther Williams
1951 *Bird of Paradise* with Louis Jourdain & Jeff Chandler
1951 *Sailor Beware* with Dean Martin & Jerry Lewis
1952 *Big Jim McLain* with John Wayne & James Arness
1953 *Hell's Half Acre*
1954 *From Here To Eternity* with Ernest Borgnine, Montgomery Clift, George Reeves, & Donna Reed
1955 *Ma and Pa Kettle At Waikiki*
1957 *Voodoo Island* with Boris Karloff

These films helped to reinforce the notion of Hawaii as a romantic place while they also stereotyped the scenic images of Diamond Head, Waikiki Beach, and Hawaiian life. Many of the best known places were shown in the films, and were subsequently included on Hawaiian fabric designs.

The Hawaii Garment Manufacturing Guild members invited Mainland department store clothing buyers to Hawaii in the 1950s and put on annual fashion shows and retail promotions. Their events led to Fashion Market Weeks, in Honolulu in 1958, 1959 and 1960, which greatly increased national and international publicity for Hawaiian garments.

Label: **Miracle Mohawk Sportswear Wash in Lukewarm Suds Press with Cool Iron.** Full color photo picture shirt of Hawaiian views. Rayon. Plastic buttons, two patch pockets. c. 1945.

Such well-known Mainland firms as Lord & Taylor, Roos Brothers, Donaldson's, Peck & Peck, Desmonds, Josky's, etc., are spending thousands of dollars of their own money advertising Hawaii. Thanks to the efforts of our Island manufacturers, everyone from Maine to Mexico as well as Canada and Cuba is becoming interested in "dressing Hawaiian." (Robyn Rickard, "Let's Dress Hawaiian," *Honolulu Star-Bulletin*, March 6, 1954, Hawaiian Life Weekly Magazine, pp. 4-5.)

'Made in Hawaii' Labels

A trade commissioner for the Los Angeles Chamber of Commerce who was visiting Hawaii in 1950 is credited with suggesting that manufacturers use a label reading 'Made in Hawaii' on their garments.

The magic words 'Made in Hawaii' can mean added dollars for Hawaii manufacturers, if they will just attach the label to the goods they produce.

The word 'Hawaii' carries with it all the enchantment of the South Seas for the average Mainlander...

Just as 'Made in Hollywood' carries with it all the glamour of the world famed film capital, and 'Made in Paris' carries with it the stamp of fashion approval.

Yet Hawaii manufacturers, with a few notable exceptions, are not taking advantage of this potential sales appeal...

Particularly, the made-in-Hawaii label would be effective on beachwear, sports clothes and aloha shirts fabricated in the islands. (*Honolulu Star-Bulletin*, April 10, 1950, Editorial Page.)

Label: None. Brown, yellow & orange "Lurline" ocean-liner design. Cotton. Coconut husk buttons. c. 1954.

The popularity of Hawaiian garments was not lost on Mainland businessmen who imitated the styles and flooded the market in the early 1950s. Companies in California particularly were producing large numbers of aloha type shirts. Therefore, use of the 'Made in Hawaii' label was repeatedly encouraged by the Hawaiian business community, and, in fact, it had a big effect on their sales.

More than half of Hawaii's sportswear production, brought once across the ocean in the form of yard goods, is shipped right back again to market.

Three things happen to the fabric to make the round trip economically profitable in the face of Mainland competition — first, before it leaves the textile plant, it is printed in an authentic and attractive island pattern; second, at home in Honolulu, it is styled in a smart and salable island fashion; and third, it is prominently labeled 'Made in Hawaii.'

The three points, in the minds of industry's leaders, are of equal importance — high praise for the magic of the Hawaiian label. (*Growing Industries for a Growing Community — Island Sportswear...Profits in Prints.* Honolulu: The Hawaiian Electric Company, Ltd., 1951, p. 8.)

...the label 'Made in Hawaii' carried immense weight in giving the buyer the feeling that he or she was walking home with a bit of the tropics tucked under the arm. (John Brosnan, "Men and Money at Work," *Honolulu Star-Bulletin*, January 31, 1953, Feature Section, p. 1.)

"Hawaiian" Becomes High Fashion

An increased emphasis on improved styling was evident as new companies entered the competition in the early 1950s and as companies already in the market sought larger volumes of Mainland sales. By 1955, the trend toward making Hawaii a resource not only for Hawaiian-Polynesian clothing but also 'high style international' clothing had begun. In the next five years, foreign markets did grow, and Hawaii worked hard to become the style center of the Pacific. (Fundaburk, Vol. II, p. 384.)

Tourism Grows

Tourism also grew rapidly in Hawaii during the 1950s as transportation costs came down. Hawaii still had the image of a rich man's destination, and so it became a status place for growing numbers of ambitious, "beautiful" people. The spectacular Moana Surfrider Hotel in Honolulu, owned by the Matson Navigation Company that also owned the luxury liner *Lurline*, opened in 1953. Aloha shirts in fabric with the *Lurline* and Moana Surfrider Hotel shown together date from this period.

Music box with a Hawaiian theme.

Label: (blue) **An Original by Hale Hawaii Made in Hawaii.** Multi-colored "chop Suey" type design with hula girls, surfers, spear fishers, kahilis, and Hawaiian words on a yellow background. Rayon. Coconut husk buttons. c. 1955.

New Fabric Prints

The prints for which Island wear is noted are a fine art within themselves.

The makers of Hawaiian garb go around like musical composers seeking fresh symphonies or like poets with eyes on the sunsets, rainbows, bays and beaches. They are constantly looking for some new print design or variation that will either catch the public fancy or create a new fashion in line and color.

One major manufacturer has a dog eared volume of lore on ancient Hawaiiana that would catch the eye of only the most ardent historian.

Yet in its reproduction of tapa designs and early Island scenes he finds the inspiration for many of the creations that have been featured in the most exclusive shops...

It requires a lucidly clear crystal ball to predict popular fancy. For example, the popularity of what the trade calls the 'chop suey' print waxes and wanes.

The chop suey print follows the general pattern of showing Diamond Head, surfboarding at Waikiki and a sprinkling of common Island words. It could be termed a 'conversation print,' because it contains a lot of words and gives the tourist something to talk about. (John Brosnan, "Men and Money at Work," *Honolulu Star-Bulletin*, January 31, 1953, Feature Section, p. 1.)

When one sees the wealth of inspiration in the fabulous flowers, trees, the underwater world, and the ancient symbols surrounding the folklore of the Islands, it is easy to understand why those prints are unique in the world. Fabric designers also draw on the Orient, as well as from the Tahitian and Polynesian cultures for ideas. (Babette, Fashion editor of the *Examiner*, "Hawaii's Apparel Industry Growing," *Los Angeles Examiner*, July 8, 1955, Sec. 2, p.4.)

Label: **The Kahala Made in Honolulu.** Brown and white tapa design with sea shells. Cotton. Coconut shell buttons. c. 1955.

A frequent example of this revamping has been the taking of the geometrical motifs from ancient tapas and combining them with shell forms or flower forms, thereby producing a variety of the popularly called 'tapas.' (Mary Howard Foster, "Hawaiian Style," *Honolulu Star-Bulletin*, April 7, 1956, Magazine Section, pp. 4-5.)

The Shirt Fabrics

Manufacturers continued to improve the fabrics they used. The quality of their colors and ease of maintenance were top priorities.

...Though as many as 10 to 14 colors can be applied simultaneously, the average number in Hawaiian prints is three or four.

By far the bulk of Hawaiian patterns are printed on cotton and the Hawaiian industry has taken-advantage of the crease-resistant finish. However, most manufacturers still prefer the regular sanforizing and mercerizing which imparts shrinkage control and greatly improves brightness of color.

Rayons are generally sold as hand-washable, the exception being Kabe crepe from Japan which ordinarily is dry cleaned.

Although some silks are sold as hand-washable, it is generally conceded that this fine cloth should be dry cleaned. The nature of the fabric is such that it has a natural crease resistance. (Mary Howard Foster, "Hawaiian Style," *Honolulu Star-Bulletin*, April 7, 1956, Magazine Section, p.5.)

Above Label: **Paradise Sports-wear Made in Hawaii.** Brown beads design on crackled background. Rayon. Coconut shell buttons. c. 1950.

Right Label: **Watumull's and Leilani made in Hawaii.** Green with brown beads design on crackled background. Rayon. Coconut shell buttons. c.1950.

Mail Order Shirts

By the mid-1950s, American mail-order catalogs were regularly carrying tropical print shirts under their own labels. These were not the expensive Hawaiian made shirts, but their own, less expensive prints in Island styles. Sears, Roebuck and Company sold shirts under the brand names Kona Kai (about 1948), Burma Gold, and Hoaloha (about 1958-1960). The Spring and Summer issue of Montgomery Ward's mail order catalog for 1957 included a "Hawaiian inspired floral print" shirt in Wash 'n Wear cotton by Fuller in three color combinations.

Hawaiian Fashion Market Weeks

In 1958, the Hawaiian Fashion Guild agreed to provide the wardrobe and sponsor the trip of "Miss Hawaii," Georgietta Kahalelaukoa Parker and a fashion consultant chaperon to the Miss America Contest in Atlantic City, New Jersey, followed by a tour of radio and television appearances and fashion shows to display Hawaiian garments in fourteen Mainland cities. The tour was highly successful, with orders for Hawaiian clothes being placed in large numbers at each show.

42

Page from the Montgomery Ward Spring & Summer mail order catalog for 1957 showing shirts of "our Hawaiian Inspired Floral Print, Wash 'n' Wear Cotton by Fuller... may be worn in or out of the trousers. Washfast."

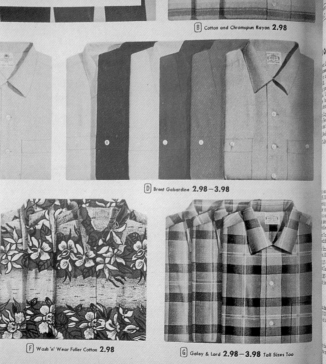

Statehood Promotes Hawaii

For a year or more before and after August 21, 1959, when Hawaii was admitted into the United States as the 50th state, Mainland stores avidly sought all things Hawaiian. Statehood cetainly boosted the importance of the 'Made in Hawaii' label.

With statehood, the name and fame of Hawaii is becoming more widespread. More headlines. More tourists. More influence in the stores throughout America. (Virginia Scallon, "Aloha Hawaii," *California Stylist*, September, 1959.)

Hawaii pennant.

43

Label: **Kihi Kihi Made in Hawaii Sportswear.** Beige background with scattered multi-colored Hawaiian monuments and lettering "49, Hawaii, Aloha, U.S.A." Rayon. Light brown plastic buttons. c. 1959. This shirt design anticipated Hawaii's becoming the 49th state in 1959. Actually, Hawaii became the 50th state, after Alaska, in 1959.

Label: **Kaikamahine Honolulu.** Red, white, and blue patterned stripes and gold shield lettered "Hawaii 50 state." Cotton. Molded bronze plastic buttons with Asian writing. c. 1959.

Label: **Shaheen's of Honolulu Made in Hawaii** (over) **Distinctive Sportswear for Discriminating People.** Red and white tapa style print and map of the Hawaiian Islands labeled, as well as lettering "50th State." Cotton. Metal buttons pressed with basket-weave design. c. 1959.

The Sixties

Fashion is that by which the fantastic becomes
for a moment universal. (Oscar Wilde)

The entertainment industry had long-since flocked to
Hawaii for recreation as well as for movie making, but in the
1960s, the emerging popular taste for more casual clothing
and life styles made Hawaii a destination for the jet-set, too.
Among the most memorable Hollywood movies featuring
Hawaii were *Waikiki Beachnik* of 1960 and *Blue Hawaii* of
1961 with Elvis Presley.

Along with the increased distribution of aloha shirts to
the U.S. Mainland after Hawaii became a state came even
more competition, especially from California. In response,
Hawaiian manufacturers developed two lines of casual shirt
styles, the now-classic Hawaiian-Polynesian style and the
new, high-fashion, Honolulu-International style. The international style shirts were made in plain as well as printed
fabrics and with strong Pacific and Far Eastern influences in
their details.

The growth the Hawaiian garment industry had experi-
enced in the 1950s resulted in Hawaiian businesses now
having local concerns more critical to their success than
establishing new overseas markets. Training programs,
protective legislation, labor relations, and retail relations all
needed overdue attention.

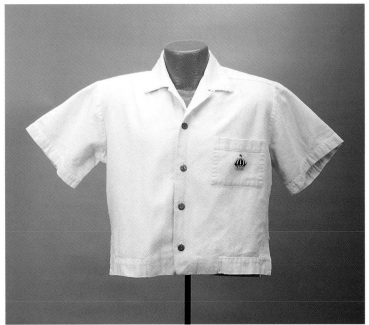

Label: **Duke Kahanamoku
Made in Hawaii by Kahala**
(separately) **Pineapple
Tweed Hawaii Sanforized
100% Cotton**. c. 1961-1965.
This shirt is solid white (no
imperfection in the yarn) and
is single stitched. An embroidered crown logo is sewn on
the patch pocket. The ma-
terial is lighter, not as coarse
as the c. 1940 pineapple
tweed that it is copying, with
a uniform slub. The collar
buttons to a loop. The collar
points are shorter, horizontal, and have no external
stitching. Large slightly con-
vex coconut shell buttons.
Cloth and shirt made by
Kahala.

45

Label: **An Authentic Hawaiian Print
Made in California Washable.** Coral
hibiscus print in five colors on a black
background. Rayon. Plastic buttons.

46

Label: **Made in Hawaii 100% cotton RN 20942.** Brown vertical panels with Asian writing. Cotton. Coconut husk buttons.

Label: **Guymont.** Multi-colored photo images and script labels of "St. Petersburg Surf Fishing Ft. Lauderdale..." Rayon. Yellow plastic buttons. Two patch pockets.

Label: **Lei-O-Hawaii Sportswear.** Orange and white rectangles with gold and black Asian writing. Cotton. Molded gold plastic round buttons. c. 1960.

The growth of Honolulu's international stature was gradually overshadowing its former individuality, and aloha shirts in the 1960s reflect this development in their more pastel and generalized fabric designs. Palm trees might appear, but not the Aloha Tower, and so forth. Companies in all the tropics, including Southern California, Florida, the Caribbean, and South America, could sell a tropical theme print better than a particularly Hawaiian print. In the early 1960s, it was apparent that the garment industry in Hawaii was not expanding at the same rate as before.

During this period, too, fashions the world over were changing to extremely casual styles, especially among students and liberal adults. Sweatshirts, T-shirts and blue jeans became the uniform of many. In the battle of casual shirt popularity, the T-shirt had won out.

Aloha shirts had been purposefully changed to appeal to a broader, international market, and in doing so, they had lost their punch. Orders did not keep up with expectations and the market, now flooded with imitations, became neutralized with mediocrity. By 1964, small Hawaiian companies could not compete.

Since many Hawaiian manufacturers could no longer support long print runs with Mainland fabric suppliers, they went elsewhere to get the cloth printed at affordable prices.

Label: **Tropical Sport Shirt by CGC Marca Registrada.** Wine red photo images and script labels of "Puerto Rico Buenos Aires Guatemala Sugar Loaf Mt. Aztec Ruins Mexico..." Rayon. Clear yellow plastic buttons. Two patch pockets.

...over 90 per cent of Hawaiian piece goods and Hawaiian designs come from Japan...Hawaiian patterns can't all be printed in New York...because New York manufacturers require a minimum order of 15,000 yards before they print one design. Who wants 15,000 yards of one pattern? Japan will print a pattern on a minimum of 3,000 yards. With smaller yardage you can use more patterns. Hawaii, easily, uses at least 1,000 patterns a year. (Ligaya Fruto, *Honolulu Star-Bulletin*, December 15, 1964, Sec. C, p. 3.)

The structure of the aloha shirt industry therefore returned to its roots. Cloth printed in Japan was once again the principal fabric chosen for aloha shirts, and gradually even their print patterns favored the Asian, rather than the American customers.

48

The Seventies and Beyond

The importance of the annual Hawaiian festivals since 1964 cannot be overstated for maintaining enthusiasm for aloha shirts. Aloha Week is held at a different time for each island, generally from mid-October to mid-November. The Merrie Monarch Festival in Hilo in April is a week-long celebration with important hula dancing competitions. In July and August, Bon Dances are Japanese traditional ceremonies. Kamehameha Day, June 11, honors the famous King, and many local festivals have continued the efforts to promote Hawaiian products in the world press.

Only the aloha shirt seems to go on forever, its only change left up to the customer — whether to wear it inside or outside the trousers. (*Island Sportswear...Profits in Prints*. 1951.)

Label: **Play Time Made in Japan.** Gray background with Asian landscapes and buildings. Rayon. Coconut husk buttons.

Label: Missing. Light blue and shaded purple background with subtle white and gray leaf design. Cotton. Clear plastic buttons. c. 1985.

Label: **Made for Surf and Shore Honolulu, Hawaii.** White with brown birds and green grass. Cotton. Coconut husk buttons.

Ceramic hula dancing girl figure, 1960s.

50

Fabric Designs

Label: (blue) **Surfriders Sportswear Manufacturers Made in Honolulu Hawaii.** Red background with multi-colored small Asian scenes and Asian writing. Rayon. Red plastic buttons. c. 1945.

Asian Designs

Label: **Watumull's and Leilani made in Hawaii** (and separately) **All Silk.** Beige with blue seahorse and shell design. Silk. Coconut husk buttons.

Label: **Duke Champion Kahanamoku An Hawaiian Original.** Dark red background with 5-color medallions and honeycomb pattern. Rayon. Oyster shell buttons. Two patch pockets. c. 1940.

Label: **McInerny's quality since 1850 Honolulu** (and separately) **Pure Silk.** Royal blue with scattered Asian objects and small dark blue leaf design. Silk. Coconut husk buttons.

52

Label: **Duke Champion Kahanamoku An Hawaiian original.** Dark green with multi-colored vignettes of figures and trees. Rayon. Oyster shell buttons. Two patch pockets. c. 1940. This is the same print as the shirt worn by Feorge Reeves as Sgt. Stork in the 1954 film *From Here To Eternity.*

Label: **Duke Champion Kahanamoku An Hawaiian Original.** Dark brown background with yellow and blue patterned circles. Rayon. Oyster shell buttons. Two patch pockets. c. 1940.

Label: **Palm Breeze Togs Hawaii.** Split leaf maple leaves and small birds against a shaded brown background. Silk. Coconut shell buttons. Long sleeves. c. 1940.

Label: **Kiilani**. Gray with yellow fishnet and red glass ball design and lettering "Mea Hoonani" (decorative) and "Popo Aniani Kalawaia" (glass fishing ball). Rayon. c. 1945.

53

Label: **National shirt shops Coast to Coast wash separately in lukewarm suds Press with cool iron - Do not starch Half Sleeves**. Pink with Asian land-scapes. Rayon. Oyster shell buttoms. c. 1948.

Label: **Duke Champion Kahanamoku Made by Cisco Unconditionally Washable.** Dark brown background with white and orange rectangular scenes and grey bamboo plants. Rayon. Oyster shell buttons. Two patch pockets. c. 1948.

Label: (large) **Duke Champion Kahanamoku Made by Cisco Unconditionally Washable.** Brown with multi-colored chrysanthemum floral design. Rayon. Oyster shell buttons. Two patch pockets and long sleeves. c. 1948.

Facing page Label: (large) **Duke Champion Kahanamoku Made by Cisco unconditionally washable.** White with blue, brown and orange chrysanthemum design. Silk. Oyster shell buttons. Two patch pockets and long sleeves. c. 1948.

Hula dancer nodding figures, 1940s, 6 1/2" high.

Label: **Coast to Coast National Shirt Shops. Wash Separately in luke-warm suds Press with cool iron - Do Not Starch Half Sleeves.** Yellow Asian landscape with figures. Rayon. Oyster shell buttons. c. 1948.

56

Label: **McInerny's quality since 1850 Honolulu** (and separately) **Pure Silk.** Gold crackled background with rectangular vignettes of Asian landscapes and brown printed fabric pieces. Silk. Coconut husk buttons. Long sleeves.

Label: **Royal Hawaiian Honolulu** (and separately) **Pure Silk Dry Clean Only.** Gray with multi-colored Asian landscape and building on stilts. Silk. Coconut husk buttons. Long sleeves. c. 1940.

Label: **Made in Hawaii**. Aqua with leaf design. Cotton. Coconut husk buttons.

Label: None. Dark yellow background with Asian landscape and growling tiger border design. Silk. Coconut husk buttons, long sleeves.

58

Label: **Flying Fish Made in Japan.** Yellow jungle scene with purple river, waterfall, and large pink growling tiger design. Rayon crepe. Coconut husk buttons.

Label: (red) **Hauoli Kamaaina Authentic Hawaiian Prints Made in California.** Dark blue background with multi-colored Asian style dragon, rickshaw, and junk design. Rayon. Black plastic buttons. Back shoulders lined with heavy wine red satin fabric. c. 1950.

Label: **Hookano Brand Made in Hawaii.** This print is known as Joss Sticks and represents boxes and loose sticks of incense. Red, black and gold on white. Silk. Coconut husk buttons, matching pocket. c. 1950-60.

Label: None. Muted colors of meandering processions of men, perhaps samurai, against a red and white geometric background with temples and mountains. Silk. Coconut shell buttons.

Labels: (red) **The Kahala Made in Honolulu** (separately) **Bullock & Jones San Francisco** (separately) **All Silk.** Blue view of Mount Fujiyama in multi-colors. Silk. Coconut shell buttons. c. 1950.

Label: **Made in Hawaii by Kahala for Andrade Resort Shop Royal Hawaiian Hotel.** Brown Asian landscape design. Silk. Coconut shell buttons. c. 1950. This is the same print as the shirt worn by John Wayne in the 1952 movie *Big Jim McLain*.

Label: **Kamehameha made and styled in Hawaii.** Red and white vertical stripes with colored circles enclosing black Hawaiian designs. Cotton. Coconut husk buttons. c. 1950.

Label: **Kamehameha made and styled in Hawaii.** Five colors, shaded pink and white floral blossoms with fans. Crepe Rayon. Coconut shell buttons. c. 1950.

Label: **Pali Hawaiian Style Hand Print.** Brown crackled background with vignettes of blue Asian landscapes. Rayon. Coconut husk buttons. Two patch pockets and long sleeves. c. 1950.

Label: **Kihi Kihi Made in Hawaii Honolulu Garment Mfg. Co.** Green with large white bird and red pine needles. Crepe Rayon. Coconut shell buttons. Two patch pockets. A dynamic design. c. 1950.

Label: **Styled by Kuhio Sportswear Honolulu Hawaii.** White with multi-colored Asian landscape and buildings. Rayon. Coconut husk buttons. c. 1952

62

Label: **Waikikian Quality Sportswear Honolulu, Hawaii.** Gray with Asian landscape vignettes. Silk. Gray plastic buttons.

"SCROLLS" HANDPRINTED IN HAWAII

Label: **Burma Gold Handprints** (over) **Made & Styled in Hawaii Exclusively for Sears.** Selvage printed: **"Scrolls" Handprinted in Hawaii.** Blue, gold, and white rectangles with Japanese style designs. Cotton. Coconut shell buttons. c. 1950.

Label: **Made in Hawaii for Andrade Resort Shops Waikiki.** Oriental designs on a tan background. Silk. Mother of pearl buttons, matching pocket, long sleeves.

63

Label: **Made in Hawaii Waikiki for Andrade Resort Shops** (and separately) **Pure Silk.** Gray crackled background with horizontal blue leaf and squares design. Silk. Coconut shell buttons.

Label: **Made in Hawaii Waikiki for Andrade Resort Shops** (separately) **Pure Silk.** Oriental designs on a blue background. Silk. Coconut shell buttons, matching pocket.

Label: **Marlboro Sportswear Washable - Use cool iron.** Grey with red, black and white bird and floral design. Rayon. Oyster shell buttons. Two patch pockets and long sleeves.

64

Label: **Pali Hawaiian Style Hand Print.** Brown with shaded red flowers, draped sticks, and geometric background with Japanese writing. Rayon. Coconut husk buttons. Two patch pockets. c. 1950.

Label: **Made in Hawaii.** Brown hookah design. Rayon. Coconut husk buttons.

65

Label: **Kramer's Honolulu Trade Mark Reg.**
Red with Asian landscape including deer.
Rayon. Coconut husk buttons. c. 1955.

Label: (red) **Malihini Made in Hawaii.**
Light green with brown leaf pattern and
Asian landscape including buildings.
Rayon. Coconut husk buttons. c. 1955.

Label: **Tropicana.** Five colors on
white with Japanese style cranes
and buildings. Rayon. Coconut
shell buttons. c. 1945-65.

66

Label: **Made in California for Richman Brothers Wash in lukewarm suds use cool iron.** Red plaid design with black patterned circles. Rayon. Red plastic buttons. Two patch pockets.

Label: **Holo-Holo Made in Hawaii.** Orange plaid with white circles enclosing Asian landscapes. Rayon crepe. Coconut husk buttons. c. 1950-60.

Label: **Holo-Holo Made in Hawaii.** Cream colored background with various multi-colored Asian implements including "One Puka Puka". The print design depicts the insignia of many Army units, perhaps in occupied Japan (1945-1952.) Rayon. Coconut husk buttons. c. 1950-60.

Label: **Hookano brand Made in Hawaii.**
Gray speckled background with brown and
multi-colored Asian objects. Silk. Coconut
husk buttons. Long sleeves. c. 1950-60.

Label: **Tru-Lustre Sportswear.** White
with red bamboo stalk and leaf design.
Rayon. White plastic buttons. Two flap
pockets and long sleeves.

Label: **Shaheen's of Honolulu** (over)
**Distinctive Sportswear for Discrimi-
nating People Made in Hawaii.** Red
and yellow patterned diamonds and
gray Thai style head with headdress.
Cotton. Coconut shell buttons. c. 1955.

68

Label: **Hawaiian Surf Made in Hawaii** (over) **Styled & Made by Pacific Sportswear Mfg. Co. Honolulu, Hawaii.** Dark brown floral design. Cotton. Coconut husk buttons. c. 1951-60.

Label: **Hoaloha made and styled in Hawaii.** Dark green with brown, blue and white Asian coins design. Silk. Molded plastic buttons with the helmeted head of a man design. c. 1960.

Label: **Alii Lole Made in Hawaii.** Cream with light brown Asian landscape. Rayon crepe. Coconut husk buttons. c. 1960.

Label: **Waikiki Sports Honolulu, Hawaii.** Brown and gray rectangular scrolls with fish and Asian writing. Cotton. Coconut shell buttons. c. 1964.

Label: Missing. Orange with Asian landscapes and figural vignettes. Rayon. Oyster shell buttons.

Label: **Capistrano Made in California.** Dark blue with Japanese style phoenix, flute and drum design. Rayon. Blue plastic buttons. Two flap pockets.

Label: **Silver of Hawaii Made in Japan.** Orange dragon on blue clouds with buildings. Rayon. Coconut husk buttons.

69

Floral Designs

70

Label: **Duke Champion Kahanamoku**. Red with white and black cotton ball design. Rayon or cotton. White buttons. c.1940.

Label: **Duke Champion Kahanamoku An Hawaiian Original.** Dark blue background with white and light blue stylized floral, fish and animal design. Rayon. Oyster shell buttons. Two patch pockets. c. 1940.

Facing page: Yellow Hawaiian leis print on a yellow background with different flower names in script, fabric yardage, Rayon, 1940s.

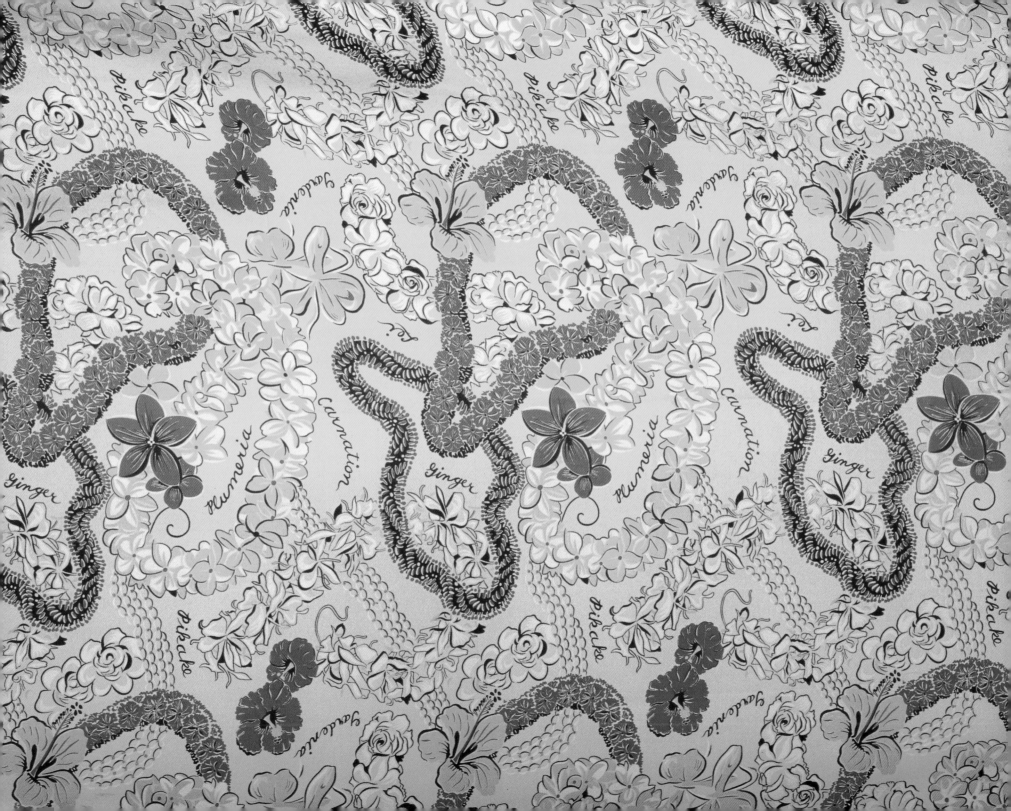

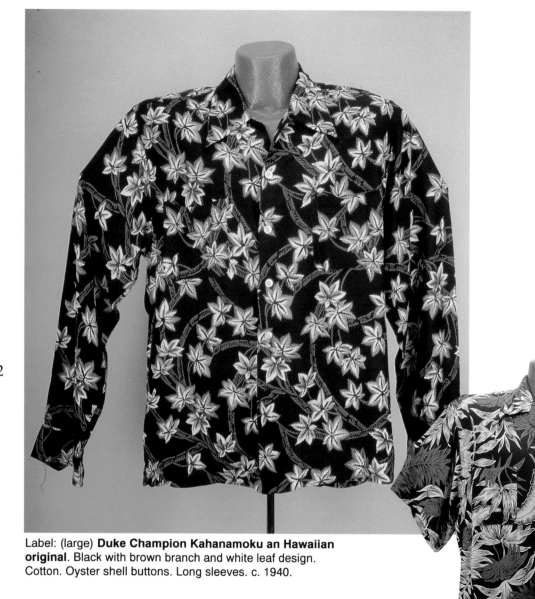

Label: (large) **Duke Champion Kahanamoku an Hawaiian original**. Black with brown branch and white leaf design. Cotton. Oyster shell buttons. Long sleeves. c. 1940.

Label: **Duke Champion Kahanamoku An Hawaiian Original**. Dark purple with green and white all-over leaf fronds. Rayon. Oyster shell buttons. Two patch pockets. c. 1940.

Label: (large) **Duke Champion Kahanamoku An Hawaiian Original**. Yellow with multi-colored vertical floral design. Rayon. Oyster shell buttons. Two patch pockets and long sleeves. c. 1940. This is the same print as a shirt worn by Montgomery Clift as Pvt. Pruitt in the 1954 movie *From Here To Eternity*.

Label: **Made in Hawaii for Ross Sutherland Honolulu**. Shaded green with white flower design. Rayon. Coconut shell buttons. c. 1940-60.

Label: **Leisure Club Sportogs**. Dark blue background with ukeleles and floral designs. Rayon. Coconut husk buttons. c. late 1940s.

Ceramic figures by Julene, 1940s, 7 1/2" high.

Label: **Bali Specially Made for Navy Exchange Guam M.I**. Flowering cactus and other plant life in multi-colors on a black background. Rayon. Plastic buttons, two patch pockets. This shirt was purchased from a man who bought it in the Pacific during the last year of World War II. He never wore it. c. 1945.

74

Label: **Kiilani Made in Honolulu.** Selvage printed: **An Original Kiilani Design "Night Blooming Cereus"**. Brown night blooming cereus floral design. Cotton. Coconut shell buttons. c. 1945.

Label: (large square) **Duke Champion Kahanamoku An Hawaiian Original**. Wine red with multi-colored floral design. Rayon. Oyster shell buttons. Two patch pockets. c. 1940.

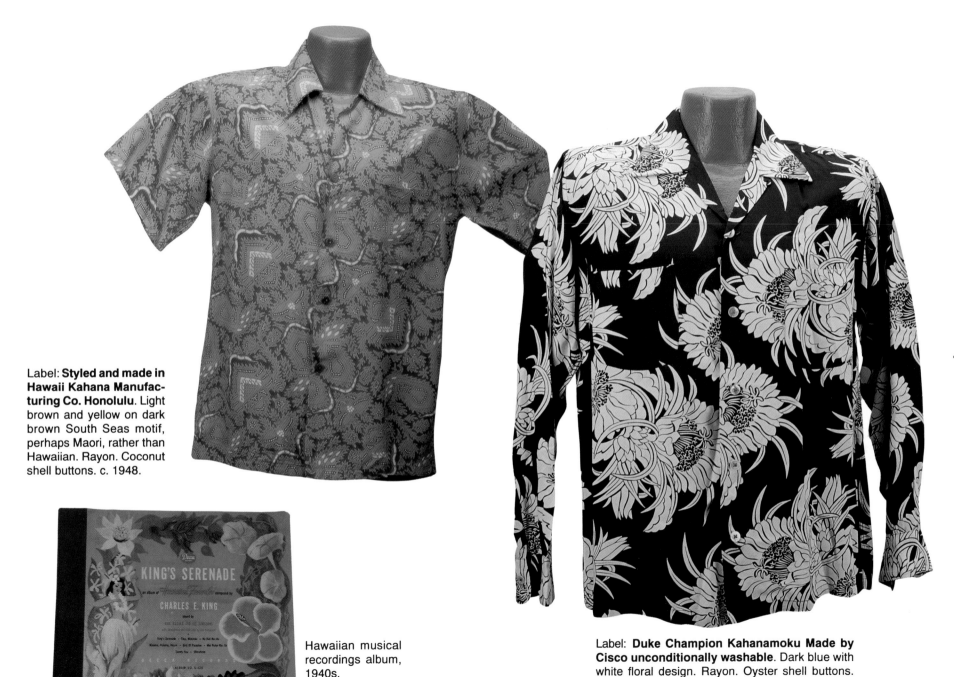

Label: **Styled and made in Hawaii Kahana Manufacturing Co. Honolulu**. Light brown and yellow on dark brown South Seas motif, perhaps Maori, rather than Hawaiian. Rayon. Coconut shell buttons. c. 1948.

Hawaiian musical recordings album, 1940s.

Label: **Duke Champion Kahanamoku Made by Cisco unconditionally washable**. Dark blue with white floral design. Rayon. Oyster shell buttons. Two patch pockets. Long sleeves. c. 1948.

Label: **Kuonakakai Authentic Hawaiian Original**. Wine red with white and green floral design and words spelled out with flowers "Hilo Kauai Maui..." Rayon. White porcelain buttons. c. 1945.

Label: **Kalakaua Made in Hawaii Rayon**. Yellow with multi-colored floral design. Rayon. Coconut husk buttons. c. 1948.

Facing page Label: **Duke Champion Kahanamoku Made by Cisco Unconditionally Washable**. White background with hibiscus and palm trees. Rayon. Oyster shell buttons. c. 1948.

Label: **Paradise Hawaii Made in Honolulu**. Red with leaf design. Cotton. Coconut shell buttons. c. 1950.

Label: (red) **The Kahala Made in Honolulu** (separately) **James McCreery & Co Fifth Avenue New York The Men's Shop**. Red with leaves and fruit of several unidentified plants in a very simple two color pattern on white cotton, double stitched. Coconut shell buttons. Slits up the side seams. c. 1950.

Label: (red) **Paradise Sportswear Made in Hawaii**. Exotic sea life print in four colors on a black background. Rayon. Coconut shell buttons. c. 1950.

Label: (green) **Kamehameha Made and Styled in Hawaii**. Selvage printed: **Kamehameha prints**. Banana leaves and flowers in multi-colors on a light brown background. Rayon. Coconut husk buttons. c. 1950.

Labels: **Made by Shaheen's of Honolulu** (separately) **Bullock's Pasadena**. Night blooming cereus design in five colors on green background. Rayon. Coconut shell buttons, two patch pockets. c. 1950.

Label: **Pali Hawaiian Style Hand Print**. Brown and multi-colored floral design. Rayon. Coconut husk buttons. Two patch pockets. c. 1950.

Label: (red block) **The Kahala Made in Honolulu**. Green with white floral design. Rayon. Coconut shell buttons. Long sleeves. c. 1950.

Label: **Pali style Hawaiian Hand Print**. Brown with shaded yellow leaf design. Cotton. Coconut shell buttons. Removable collar stays. c. 1950.

Label: **Kuu-Ipo Made in Hawaii**. Blue with white shells and vine design. Rayon. Coconut husk buttons. c. 1951.

Label: **Hale Niu Honolulu**. Red and multi-colored floral design. Cotton. Coconut shell buttons. c. 1950.

Label: (large) **Iolani Made in Hawaii**. Ten pastel colors in floral print with mountain landscape and large red flowers. Crepe Rayon. Coconut husk buttons. c. 1955.

Label: **The Liberty House Honolulu Waikiki**. Ten color floral print with mountain landscape and large red flowers. Crepe Rayon. Coconut shell buttons.

Label: **Made in California washable**. Brown with four-color leis, flowers, palm tree, and lettering "Aloha Hawaii." Rayon. Brown plastic buttons, two flap pockets.

82

Label: **Lauhala**. Brown with large white and yellow floral design. Rayon. Coconut shell buttons. c. 1955.

Label: **An original by Hale Hawaii Made in Hawaii**. Wine red with white and gray tree limb design. Rayon. Coconut husk buttons. Long sleeves. c. 1955.

Label: (small) **Iolani Made in Hawaii**. Yellow with blue leaf pattern. Crepe Rayon. Coconut husk buttons. c. 1955.

Label: **Hawaiian Casuals by Stan Hicks Made in Honolulu**. Blue with purple floral pattern on black crackled background. Silk. Molded plastic buttons with the helmeted head of a man design. Long sleeves. c. 1955.

83

Label: (brown) **Made in Hawaii for Andrade Resort Shops Waikiki**. Cascading yellow orchids on purple background. Rayon. Coconut shell buttons.

Label: **An Original by Hale Hawaii Made in Hawaii**. Brown with four-color floral print including yellow orchids. Rayon. Coconut shell buttons. c. 1955.

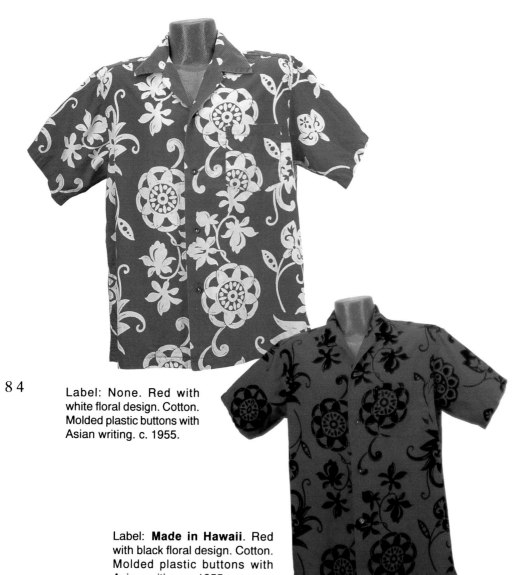

84

Label: None. Red with white floral design. Cotton. Molded plastic buttons with Asian writing. c. 1955.

Label: **Made in Hawaii**. Red with black floral design. Cotton. Molded plastic buttons with Asian writing. c. 1955.

Label: None. Red with white floral design. Cotton. Molded plastic buttons with Asian writing. c. 1955.

Label: **alfred Shaheen Honolulu**. Red with white leaf design. Cotton. Molded plastic buttons with Asian writing. c. 1955.

Label: (rainbow colored) **Tropicool Sportswear**. Green with four-color floral design. Rayon. White plastic buttons. Two patch pockets.

Label: **Made in Hawaii by Kahala for Andrade Resort Shop Royal Hawaiian Hotel**. Blue with white vertical floral design. Cotton. Coconut shell buttons. c. 1955.

Label: **Hookano Brand Made in Hawaii**. Selvage printed: **Textile Company of America © "Prints of the Seven Seas."** Blue with yellow figs. Cotton. Coconut husk buttons. c. 1950-60.

Label: **Manhattan Washable**. Brown with white leaf design. Rayon. Oyster shell buttons. Two flap pockets.

8 6

Label: (blue) **Made in Hawaii 100% Cotton RN 20942**. Royal blue with white floral design. Cotton. Molded plastic buttons with Asian writing.

Label: **Balsam**. Blue with white leaf design. Rayon. Oyster shell buttons. Two flap pockets.

Label: **Jantzen Made in U.S.A.**
Yellow floral design. Rayon.
Coconut shell buttons.

Ceramic Hawaiian figurines,
5 1/2" high, 3 1/2" high.

Label: **The Kahala Made in Honolulu**. Gray
and yellow ocean plant design in rectangular
blocks. Cotton. Coconut shell buttons. c. 1955.

88

Label: **Jantzen Made in U.S.A.**
Wine red with black and white floral design. Heavy ribbed Rayon.
Red shell buttons. Two waist patch pockets.

Ming's of Honolulu.
Plumeria flower pin. Ivory.
c. 1950.

Label: **Surf 'n Sand made in Honolulu, Hawaii** (over) **Distinctive Sportswear for Discriminating People Made in Hawaii.**
Brown and yellow floral design. Cotton.
Coconut shell buttons. c. 1955.

Label: **Nani Honolulu**.
Dark blue with white leis
design. Cotton. Coconut
shell buttons. c. 1950-60.

Label: **Mark Twain**. Brown with
pink and blue leis and ukelele
design. Rayon. White buttons.

Label: **Surfriders Sportswear Manufacturers
Made in Honolulu Hawaii**. White with three-color
floral design and crackled background. Cotton.
Molded plastic buttons with Asian writing. c. 1955.

Label: (black) **Made in Hawaii 100% Cotton RN 20942**. Dark mottled pink background with white, purple, and brown spotted leaves. Cotton. Metal buttons. c. 1960s.

Label: (green) **kona*kai Hawaiian Casuals made in U.S.A. by jantzen**. Red with white stylized floral design. Cotton. Plastic buttons. c. 1960.

Label: **Trade Wind Fashions The Liberty House Waikiki On the Beach at Waikiki Honolulu, Hawaii**. White background with four-color vertical bird of paradise, philodendron monstera, and plumeria print. Rayon. Coconut shell buttons, two matching pockets.

Label: **Maile -Sanforized- R 100% cotton RN 17807 Made in Japan**. Red tapa design overlaid with white flowers. Cotton. Coconut husk buttons. c. 1960.

Label: None. Selvage printed: **"Plumeria" Surf n' Sand Handprint - Hawaii**. Blue with yellow and white plumeria floral design. Cotton. Coconut shell buttons. c. 1955.

Label: **Kona Kai made in Hawaii for Sears**. Black with brown and blue leaves and scattered flowers. Cotton. Coconut husk buttons. c. 1960.

Label: **Ashfield Made in California by Duke of Hollywood Co.** Dark blue with multi-colored floral design. Rayon. Dark blue shell buttons. Two flap pockets.

Label: **Grosdale Sportswear**. Dark blue background with red floral design. Rayon. Gray shell buttons. Two flap pockets and long sleeves.

Label: **Kona Kai made in Hawaii for Sears**. White with brown and green floral design. Cotton. Coconut husk buttons. c. 1960.

93

Label: **Del Mar Sportswear Made in California**.
Yellow with multi-colored floral design. Rayon.
Yellow plastic buttons. Two flap pockets.

94

Label: **Pikaki Made in Hawaii**. Brown with large white Hibiscus flowers. Rayon. Coconut husk buttons. c. 1964.

Label: **Pikaki Made in Hawaii**. Gray with red and turquoise floral design. Cotton. Coconut husk buttons. c. 1964.

Label: (red italics) **Kamehameha made and styled in Hawaii**. White and beige background with red floral design. Cotton. Metal clad molded buttons with King Kamehameha figure and lettering "Kamehameha." c. 1960.

95

Label: (red italics) **Kamehameha made and styled in Hawaii**. Chartreuse with red and green fern design. Cotton. Coconut husk buttons. c. 1960.

Label: (red italics) **Kamehameha made and styled in Hawaii**. Orange and pink floral design. Cotton. Metal clad buttons with impressed King Kamehameha image and lettering "Kamehameha." c. 1960.

96

Label: (red) **Made in Hawaii**. Multi-colored green and brown stylized frog and blue floral design in vertical arrangement. Rayon. Coconut husk buttons.

Label: (red) **Made in Hawaii**. Multi-colored blue and pink stylized frog and green floral design in vertical arrangement. Rayon. Coconut husk buttons.

Label: (folded & black) **Malihini Made in Hawaii**. Brown and green all-over floral design. Silk. Coconut husk buttons. c. 1960.

Label: **Dr. Beach TM Made in USA of imported fabric over for care**. Blue with large green leaves and red hibiscus design. Rayon. Very recent.

97

Label: None. White with red leaf design. Cotton. Coconut shell buttons.

Label: **Network**. Red with yellow and blue leaves and boats. Rayon. Plastic buttons. c. 1970.

Label: **Network**. Blue with color-ful rainbow and flowers. Rayon. Plastic buttons. c. 1970.

98

Label: **Paradise Found Honolulu Hawaii**. Red with colorful floral design. Cot-ton. Coconut husk buttons. c. 1970.

Label: (black) **Made in Hawaii**. Bright pink, red, and purple flo-ral design. Polyester. White buttons. c. 1970s.

Label: **Pennshire Sportswear for leisure**. Peach with multi-colored bird of paradise floral design. Rayon. Off-white plastic buttons. Two patch pockets.

Label: **Shapely Hand Washable by Mack**. Yellow with white and gray leaf design. Rayon. Yellow plastic buttons. Two patch pockets.

Label: None. Dark pink and white stylized fruit and floral design. Cotton. Coconut shell buttons.

Label: **Hana Maui Shop**. Green background with white leaf design. Cotton. Coconut shell buttons.

100

Label: (large) **National Shirt Shops**. Green with palm tree design. Rayon. White plastic buttons. Two patch pockets. c. 1948.

Miniature ceramic figurines, 1950s.

Label: (large) **National Shirt Shops**. Dark blue with yellow palm design. Rayon. White plastic buttons. Two patch pockets. c. 1948.

Label: **Random Wear Authentically styled**. Beige with palm stalks and leaves. Rayon. White plastic buttons. Two flap pockets and long sleeves.

Label: **Arrow Made in U.S.A. "Sanforset" Rayon**. White with multi-colored palm tree and water-fall design. Rayon. Oyster shell buttons. Two flap pockets.

Label: (large) **National Shirt Shops**. Dark blue with multi-colored palm tree and stalks. Rayon. White plastic buttons. Two patch pockets. c. 1948.

Label: (large) **National Shirt Shops**. White with blue bamboo cane and palm branch design. Rayon. White plastic buttons. Two patch pockets. c. 1948.

Label: **Penney's Topflight Hand Washable**. Red with yellow palm tree and stalks. Rayon. Red plastic buttons. Two patch pockets. c. 1950.

Label: **Penney's Topflight Hand Washable Rayon**. White with green pineapple and palm tree design. Rayon. White plastic buttons. Two patch pockets. c. 1950.

Label: **Duke Champion Kahanamoku An Hawaiian Original**. Dark blue with white palm tree and moon design. Rayon. Oyster shell buttons. Two patch pockets. c. 1940.

103

Label: **Duke Champion Kahanamoku Made By Cisco**. Wine red border print of landscape, palm trees, and figures. Rayon. Oyster shell buttons. Two patch pockets. c. 1948

104

Label: **Duke Champion Kahanamoku Made By Cisco**. Dark blue with multi-colored palm trees border print. Rayon. Oyster shell buttons. Two patch pockets. c. 1948.

Label: **Duke Champion Kahanamoku Made By Cisco**. Brown with multi-colored palm trees border print. Rayon. Oyster shell buttons. Two patch pockets. c. 1948.

Fruit Designs

Label: **Royal Palm Tampa, Fla.** Cream with oranges, grapefruit, limes, and lemons. Rayon. White plastic buttons.

Label: (blue) **Made in Hawaii**. Green with white palm leaf and very stylized figures in black and yellow. Rayon. Coconut husk buttons.

Label: **Arrow Made in U.S.A. Washable**. Cream with green fan palm design. Rayon. Gray plastic buttons. Two flap pockets.

Label: **Duke Champion Kahanamoku An Hawaiian Original**. Dark green with yellow grapefruits and white leaves. Rayon. Oyster shell buttons. Two patch pockets. c. 1940.

Labels: **Washington Shirt Co. Sportswear** (separately) **Hawaiian Prints**. White with four-color floral and banana bunch design. Rayon. Yellow plastic buttons.

Label: **The Kahala Made in Honolulu for M. McInerny**. White with multi-colored, horizontal, labeled cocktails. Cotton. Molded plastic bamboo-shaped buttons. c. 1955-60.

Label: **Made in Hawaii for Ross Sutherland Honolulu**. Orange with border print of multi-colored cocktails and labels. Cotton. Molded plastic buttons with Asian writing. c. 1940-60.

Label: **Duke Champion Kahanamoku An Hawaiian Original**. Dark green with white pineapple pattern. Rayon. Oyster shell buttons. Two patch pockets. c. 1940. This is the same print as a shirt worn by Ernest Borgnine as Sgt. Judson in the 1954 movie *From Here To Eternity*.

Label: Missing. Dark brown with white pineapple pattern. Rayon. Oyster shell buttons. Two patch pockets.

Label: **Duke Champion Kahanamoku Made by Cisco unconditionally washable**. Dark blue with white pineapple design and white terry cloth lining. Cotton. Large oyster shell buttons. Two waist patch pockets. c. 1948.

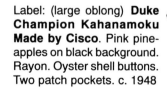

Label: (large oblong) **Duke Champion Kahanamoku Made by Cisco**. Pink pineapples on black background. Rayon. Oyster shell buttons. Two patch pockets. c. 1948

Label: (small oblong) **Duke Champion Kahanamoku Made by Cisco Unconditionally Washable**. Purple pineapples on black background. Rayon. Oyster shell buttons. Two patch pockets. c. 1948.

Label: **harper**. Yellow with red pineapples and blue lettering of Hawaiian place names. Rayon. Yellow plastic buttons. c. 1950s.

Label: (green) **Malihini Made in Hawaii**. Pineapple design with blue background. Rayon. c. 1955.

Label: **Tropicals Washable**. Dark blue with four-color pineapple design. Rayon. White plastic buttons.

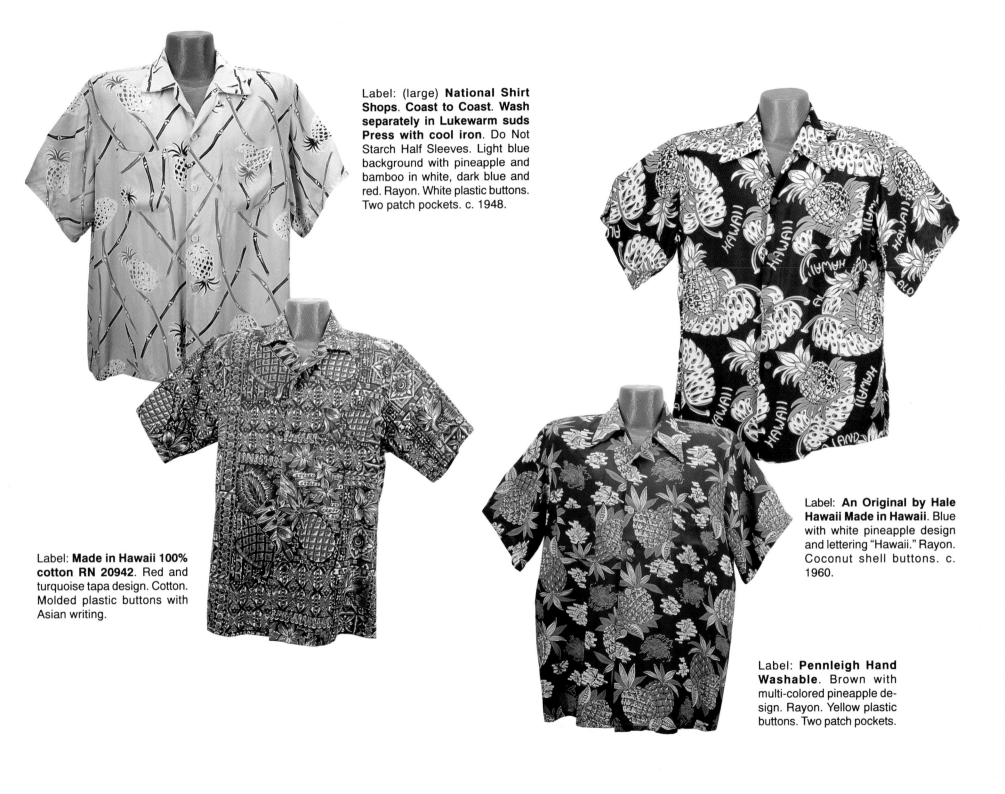

Label: (large) **National Shirt Shops. Coast to Coast. Wash separately in Lukewarm suds Press with cool iron**. Do Not Starch Half Sleeves. Light blue background with pineapple and bamboo in white, dark blue and red. Rayon. White plastic buttons. Two patch pockets. c. 1948.

Label: **Made in Hawaii 100% cotton RN 20942**. Red and turquoise tapa design. Cotton. Molded plastic buttons with Asian writing.

Label: **An Original by Hale Hawaii Made in Hawaii**. Blue with white pineapple design and lettering "Hawaii." Rayon. Coconut shell buttons. c. 1960.

Label: **Pennleigh Hand Washable**. Brown with multi-colored pineapple design. Rayon. Yellow plastic buttons. Two patch pockets.

110

Label: **Made by Shaheen's of Honolulu** (over) **Distinctive Sportswear for Discriminating People Made in Hawaii**. Blue Floral and pineapple design. Cotton. Coconut shell buttons. c. 1955.

Label: **The Liberty House Honolulu Waikiki**. Green with pineapple pattern over crackled background. Rayon. Coconut husk buttons.

Label: **Made by Shaheen's of Honolulu** (over) **Distinctive Sportswear for Discriminating People Made in Hawaii**. Brown tapa, pineapple and hibiscus design, this hand print is known as "Hawaiian Paradise" and was printed by Surf 'n Sand, a Shaheen company. Cotton, double stitched. Coconut shell buttons. c. 1955.

Pineapple salt and pepper shakers: Tilted pair 2" high, In basket 4" high, Standing pair 3 1/2" high.

Label: **Hawaii Blues** (separately) **100% Polynosic Rayon RN 11935 Made in Korea See rev. for care**. Yellow with green leaves and purple pineapples. Rayon. Plastic buttons. Recent.

Label: **Hilo Hattie Made in Hawaii**. Beige background with pineapple, travel brochures, and floral design along with words "Waikiki," and "Pacific." Cotton. Small coconut shell buttons. c. 1985.

Hawaiian Motifs

Black "Hawaiian Chant Hula" fabric yardage. Rayon. 1940s.

112

Gray Hawaiian motifs fabric yardage with lettering of Hawaiian place names. Rayon. 1940s.

113

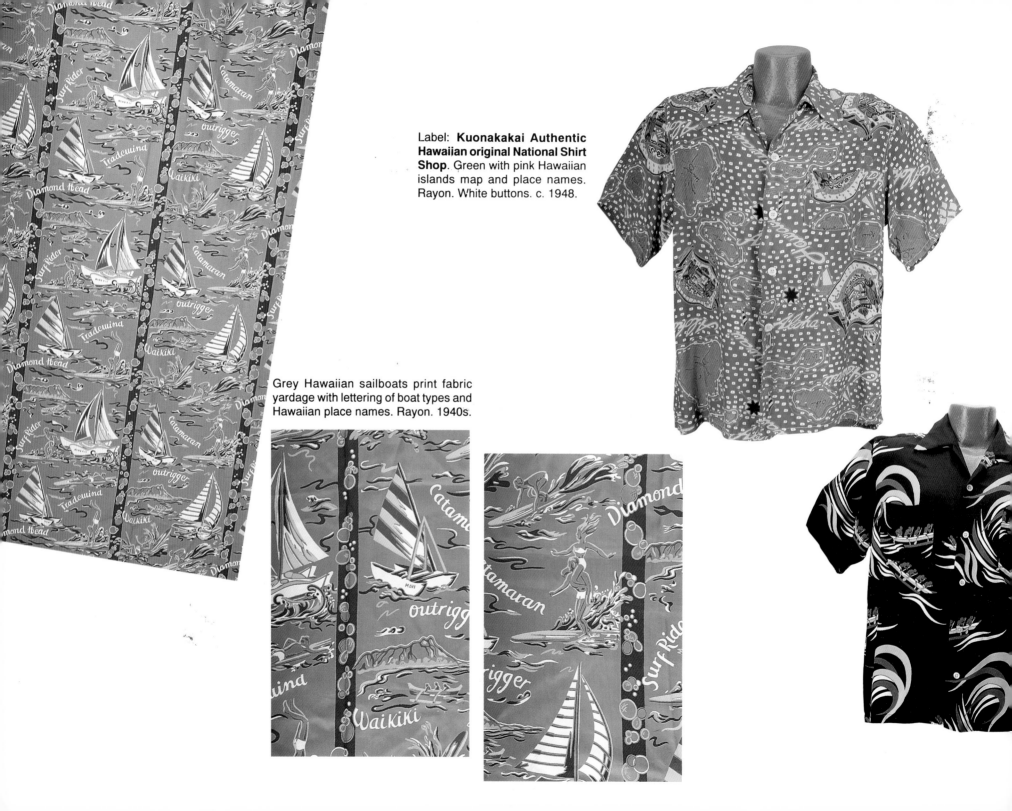

Label: **Kuonakakai Authentic Hawaiian original National Shirt Shop**. Green with pink Hawaiian islands map and place names. Rayon. White buttons. c. 1948.

Grey Hawaiian sailboats print fabric yardage with lettering of boat types and Hawaiian place names. Rayon. 1940s.

Label: **Surf 'n Sand made in Honolulu, Hawaii** (over) **Distinctive Sportswear for Discriminating People Made in Hawaii**. Brown with silver and gold printed and labeled shipping lines map of the Hawaiian islands. Cotton. Coconut husk buttons. c. 1955.

Label: **Poinciana Sportswear**. Rust with the Hawaiian Islands labeled and Hawaiian vignettes. Rayon. White plastic buttons. Two patch pockets.

Label: **Duke Champion Kahanamoku An Hawaiian Original**. Dark blue with multi-colored men in an outrigger canoe design. Rayon. Oyster shell buttons. Two patch pockets. c. 1940.

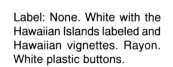

Label: None. White with the Hawaiian Islands labeled and Hawaiian vignettes. Rayon. White plastic buttons.

Labels: (red) **Made in California Don Juan of California Wash in luke warm suds Press with cool iron (separately) acetate and nylon**. Solid light yellow with brown surfing boy printed on the back. Nylon. Oyster shell buttons and two flap pockets.

Salt and pepper shaker hula dancing girls and pam trees.

Label: **Capistrano reg'd by Wismar Made in California**. Red with a large Caucasian maiden in island dress and flowers design printed on the back. The floral design is on the front pocket and collar. Front and long sleeves are solid red. Rayon. Oyster shell buttons. c. 1940s.

117

Label: **harper Sportswear**. Red with multi-colored drums and palm branches. Rayon. White plastic buttons. c. late 1940s.

Label: **Duke Champion Kahanamoku Made by Cisco**. Dark blue with white dots and five-color vignettes of Hawaiian images. Rayon. Oyster shell buttons. c. 1948.

Label: **Aloha Kanaka Original by Artvogue**. Black background with pink and green design of three hula dancers at the centers of three flowers and white lettering "Hawaii." Rayon. Black plastic buttons.

118

Label: **Surf 'n Sand Made in Honolulu, Hawaii**. Red with gold and silver volcanoes design. Cotton. Metal buttons impressed with basket-weave design. c. 1955.

Label: **Hoaloha Made and styled in Hawaii**. Red with silver and gold volcano design. Cotton. Coconut buttons. c. 1960.

Label: **Kulani Beach Tropical Sportswear**. Yellow with multi-colored Keoni surfboard design. Rayon. Oyster shell buttons. Two patch pockets. c. 1940.

Label: **McInerny's Quality since 1850 Honolulu**. White with brown horizontal hula dancer illustrations, words to the song "Lovely Hula Hands," bars of musical notes and the ukulele chords. Cotton. Coconut shell buttons.

Label: **McInerny's Quality Since 1850 Honolulu**. Red with volcanos and figural carvings design. Cotton. Coconut husk buttons.

119

Label: None. Dark blue with feather ornaments and script writing including "Hawaii." Blue plastic buttons.

Label: **Golden Gate Made in California 100% Nylon**. White with red and blue pineapple, ukulele, and Hawaiian place names design. Very thin and transparent ribbed nylon. White plastic buttons.

Label: (script) **The Kahala Made in Honolulu**. Brown with figures and surf boards design. Cotton. Coconut shell buttons. c. 1955. *See same fabric design in The Fifties section.*

120

Label: (large) **The Kahala made in Honolulu for M. McInerny**. Red with scattered figures in black and white. Cotton. Molded silver colored plastic buttons with the head of a man and labeled "Hawaii." c. 1955.

Label: **Hoaloha Made and styled in Hawaii**. Dark blue with multi-colored Hawaiian insignia, labeled "Tiki Hibiscus Hula..." Cotton. Coconut husk buttons. c. 1960.

Label: **An Original by Hale Hawaii Made in Hawaii**. Dark turquoise with black and gold boat paddles design. Coconut shell buttons. c. 1955.

Label: **Malihini Made in Hawaii**. White with red paddles design. Cotton. Coconut shell buttons. C. 1955.

121

Label: Missing. Blue and red vignettes of sailboats and hula dancers labeled "Ala Moana (By the Sea)." Cotton. Coconut shell buttons.

Label: **Shaheen's of Honolulu Made in Hawaii**. White with multi-colored Hawaiian images, red fez marked "Aaonms," dagger, and lettering "Aloha." Cotton. Molded plastic buttons with basket-weave pattern. Long sleeves. c. 1950-55.

122

Label: **Tailored by Imperial Trade Mark**. Water sports and Waikiki landmarks in four colors on blue background and with white lettering "Waikiki." Rayon. Plastic buttons, two patch pockets. Note original button tag. c. 1950.

Label: **Pali Hawaiian Style Hand Print**. Mountain landscape with anthurium and pineapples on white background. Rayon. Coconut husk buttons. c. 1950.

Label: **Styled by Kuhio Sportswear Honolulu Hawaii**. Red with multi-colored carved paddles design. Rayon. Coconut husk buttons. Long sleeves. c. 1952.

Label: (large) **Surf 'n Sand Made in Honolulu, Hawaii**. Colorful yellow, red, and green uli uli on a black background. Rayon. Coconut shell buttons, two flapped pockets, long sleeves. The uli uli, or feathered gourd rattle, is used in some forms of the hula. c. 1955.

Label: (small) **Surf 'n Sand Made in Honolulu Hawaii**. Colorful yellow, red and green uli uli on a black background. Rayon. This shirt is styled differently. Coconut shell buttons, two patch pockets, short sleeves. c. 1955.

Uli Uli rattle, 10" long.

Label: **Polynesian Sportswear Made in Hawaii**. White with multi-colored mountain landscape and sporting figures. Rayon crepe. Coconut husk buttons. c. 1955.

Label: **Kihi Kihi Made in Hawaii Sportswear**. Land of Aloha novelty print in five colors on black background. Rayon. Plastic buttons. c. 1955.

124

Label: (small) **The Kahala Made in Honolulu for M. McInerny**. White with multi-colored horizontal design of Hawaiian figures and labels. Cotton. Leather buttons stamped with pineapple design. c. 1955.

Label: (blue) **An Original by Hale Hawaii Made in Hawaii** (with grass shack and palm tree). Land of Aloha novelty print in five colors on green background. Rayon. Coconut shell buttons. c. 1955.

Label: none. Land of Aloha type of multicolor print. Rayon crepe. Coconut husk buttons.

Label: **Original by Hale Hawaii Made in Hawaii**. Land of Aloha type of multi-color print. Rayon. Coconut husk buttons, matching pocket. c. 1955.

Label: **Central Pacific Importers of Hawaii Made in Japan**. Orange landscape with surf riders and Aloha Tower. Rayon. Coconut husk buttons.

Label: (green) **Hoomaha Made and styled in Hawaii**. Black background with colorful hula girls and lettering "Do the hula little brown gal on the beach at Waikiki hula hands Hawaiian hospitality hula lovely aloha." Rayon. Black plastic buttons.

Label: **Pacific Made in Honolulu**. Novelty shirt with Hawaiian words and phrases, Kamehameha statue, hula girls, surfers in three colors on a white background. Rayon. White plastic buttons. c. 1951-60.

Label: **Holo-Holo Made in Hawaii**. Red with multi-colored flowers and implements. Crepe Rayon. Coconut husk buttons. c. 1950-60.

Label: **Made in California Westwood Casuals Klein-Norton Co.** Green with white flowers and ukulele-shaped vignettes filled with five-color people in water activities. Rayon. Green plastic buttons. Two patch pockets.

Scenic Designs

Label: **Kulani Beach Tropical Sportswear**. Blue background with island scenes and lettering "Around Hawaii." Rayon. Oyster shell buttons. Two patch pockets. c. 1940.

128

Label: None. Anonymous tailor made. White with red leis, hula girls, palm trees and calabashes. Rayon. Plastic buttons, size tag clipped from collar. c. 1935.

Label: (red) **Kuonakakai authentic Hawaiian originals**. Red background with blue, green, and yellow tropical scenes and lettering including "Halekulani Hotel" and "Molokai." Rayon. White buttons. Special shirt. c. 1945.

Label: **Sportswear Made in California for Macy's Men's Store**. Dark blue with grass hut marked "Trader" and South Seas place names. Rayon. Coconut shell buttons. Long sleeves. c. 1940s.

Label: **Campus**. Blue background with volcanoes and canoes in vignettes. Rayon. Blue plastic buttons. c. 1940s.

Figural Okolehao liquor bottles, 6" high.

Label: (large) **Duke Champion Kahanamoku An Hawaiian Original**. Dark blue with boats design. Rayon. White buttons. Folded as sold with original tags. c.1940.

Label: **Waikiki Originals The Liberty House Waikiki on the Beach at Waikiki Honolulu, Hawaii**. Dark brown background with multi-colored design of Honolulu places and labels including "Ala Moana Park, Native beach umbrellas, "Ala Moana" (road by the ocean), Hawaii…" Rayon. Coconut shell buttons, two patch pockets.

Label: **Alpine sportswear Inc. Dallas** (over) **Hand Washable Use Cool Iron**. Yellow background with multi-colored vignettes of Hawaiian woman with fruit tray, men in sailboat, palm trees, and flowers. Rayon. Oyster shell buttons, two flap pockets with buttons, long sleeves.

131

Label: **Pohaku Made in Hawaii**. Magnificent net fishermen print in ten colors. Rayon. Coconut husk buttons. One perfectly matched pocket.

Label: (red) **Styled and Made in Hawaii Kahana Manufacturing Co. Honolulu**. Red background with multi-colored Hawaiian people including helmeted warrior and maidens with flowers and fruit. Rayon. Coconut shell buttons. c. 1948.

Label: (blue) **Surfriders Sportswear Manufacturers Made in Honolulu Hawaii**. Dark brown background with yellow and green scattered vignettes of Hawaiian native life including the Royal Coat of Arms. Rayon. Brown plastic buttons. c. 1945.

Label: (yellow block) **Made in Hawaii by Kahala for Andrade Resort Shop Royal Hawaiian Hotel**. Selvage printed: **Royal Hawaiian - Kahala Prints - Designed and Created in Honolulu**. Yellow with six-color design of tourists, hula girls, lei sellers, script lettering "Wai Lae Country club," "Aloha Towers," "Lei Sellers," "S. S. *Lurline*." and other Hawaiian place names as well as "Matson Lines" on a gang plank railing. Rayon. Coconut shell buttons. c. 1953.

Label: **Pali Hawaiian Style Made in Hawaii**. Brown with light brown line drawings of mountains, net fishermen, surfers, men in boat and vignettes in the shapes of the islands filled with multi-colored landscape scenes with landmarks. Rayon. Coconut husk buttons. c. 1950.

Label: **Pali Hawaiian Style**. Savage-inspired print. Rayon crepe. Coconut buttons and matching pocket. This is a special shirt because of the great color saturation. c. 1950.

Label: **Made in Hawaii**. Brown background with lettering "Aloha" and the aloha tower in Honolulu. Rayon crepe. Coconut husk buttons. c.1950s.

Label: **Pali Style Hawaiian**. Multi-color surfers, net casters, guitars, malolo, and tropical foliage. Rayon. Coconut husk buttons. Two matching pockets, single stitched. c. 1955. This is a forty year old reproduction of a fifty year old shirt. Note that the rayon is not crepe.

Label: **Original by Hale Hawaii Made in Hawaii**. Multi-color surfers, net casters, guitars, malolo, and tropical foliage. Rayon crepe. Coconut husk buttons. Matching pocket. c. 1955.

134

Label: (green) **Hale Hawaii Made in Hawaii**. Medium blue background with multi-colored Hawaiian figures and palm trees with lettering. Rayon. Coconut husk buttons. c. 1951.

Labels: (blue) **Made in Hawaii**. Selvages printed: **Kamehameha print**. On both shirts, boys climbing coconut trees with waiting girls and brilliant sunset printed in multi-colors on a medium blue background on one shirt and a black background on the other. Rayon. Coconut husk buttons. c. 1950.

Label: (green with palm trees and ocean) **Made in Hawaii**. Selvage printed: **Kamehameha prints**. Dark blue background with green, orange and gray design lettered "Noa Noa" of native people in the manner of artist Paul Gauguin's drawings of Tahiti. This design is attributed to John Miegs. c. 1950.

Label: **Made in Hawaii for Hawaiian Sport Shop Inc. Ft. Lauderdale, Surfside, Florida**. Vibrant landscape with outrigger canoe. Crepe Rayon. Coconut husk buttons. Long sleeves. c. 1945.

Label: **Kilohana Made in Hawaii**. Green background with many colorful scenes of Hawaii including "Aloha Tower" and other lettering. Rayon. Coconut shell buttons. Special shirt. c. 1954.

Label: (green) **Malihini Made in Hawaii**. Black background with multi-colored scenes of native Hawaiian people in island clothing and white lettering labels. Rayon. White plastic buttons and long sleeves. c. 1955.

136

Label: **McGregor Made in U.S.A. Washable**. Sailboats on a black and red sea. Rayon. Oyster shell buttons. c. 1950.

Label: **Pali Hawaiian Styled Hand Print 100% Rayon**. Vibrant landscape with outrigger canoe and flowers. Rayon. White plastic buttons. c. 1950.

Label: **An Original by Hale Hawaii Made in Hawaii**. Multi-colored Hawaiian activities against a shaded brown ocean. Rayon. Coconut husk buttons. c. 1955.

Label: (red) **Malihini Made in Hawaii**. The design, lettered "Hoonanea," is in five colors and depicts pleasant activities (hoonanea) near four different island trees: a luau around the breadfruit, doing the hula to the accompaniment of a ukulele under the banyan, lei making beside the plumeria, and lauhala mat weaving beneath the hala. Rayon. Coconut husk buttons. c. 1955.

138

Label: (green) **Malihini Made in Hawaii**. Black background with yellow, orange, and gray design of hula girls, flowers, Royal Coat of Arms, and lettering. Rayon. Coconut shell buttons. c. 1955.

Label: (blue) **Made in Hawaii**. Blue with vignettes of Hawaiian scenes including Aloha Tower and script "Aloha Hawaii, Hawaii the Alohaland, Aloha, Land of Aloha." Rayon. Coconut husk buttons.

Label: **Made in Hawaii by Iolani**. Red and gray volcanic beach with blue ferns. Rayon. Coconut husk buttons. c. 1955.

Label: None. Selvage printed: **Surf 'n Sand Hand Prints Ltd. Honolulu, Hawaii**. Dark blue and white plantation design. Cotton. Coconut shell buttons. c. 1955.

Label: (blue) **An original "Poi Pounder Tog" Hawaiian Togs - Honolulu**. Dark brown background with multi-colored design including Diamond head, surfing scene, lei seller, dancers and lettering of many phrases including "Surfing at Waikiki," "Hawaii," and "Flowers and Fruit of Alohaland." Rayon. Coconut shell buttons. c. 1955.

Label: **Pali Style**. Beautiful green seascape with arch in the rock, island, mountain and flowers. Rayon. Coconut husk buttons.

140

Label: **An Original by Hale Hawaii Made in Hawaii**. Multi-colored landscape with rainbow. Crepe Rayon. Coconut husk buttons. c. 1955.

Label: **Hale Hawaii Made in Hawaii**. Red, green, blue and grey on white with Matson Lines, Royal Hawaiian Band, Don the Beachcomber designs. Rayon. Coconut shell buttons. c. 1951.

Label: **Original by Hale Hawaii**. Multi-colored landscape with waterfall and rainbow. Crepe Rayon. Coconut shell buttons. c. 1955.

Label: **Hale Hawaii Made in Hawaii**. Blue and grey on white with Matson Lines, Royal Hawaiian Band, Don the Beachcomber designs. Rayon. Coconut shell buttons. c. 1951.

Label: **Kilohana Made in Hawaii**. Brown and yellow *Lurline* oceanliner design. Cotton. Coconut husk buttons. c. 1954.

141

Label: **Surf 'n Sand made in Hawaii for Andrade Resort Shops** (over) **The Royal Hawaiian Hotel and Moana Surf Rider Hotel on the beach at Waikiki** (and separately) **Pure Silk**. Brown *Lurline* oceanliner design. Silk. Coconut shell buttons. Long sleeves. c. 1954.

Label: **Alii Lole Made in Hawaii**. Red *Lurline* oceanliner design. Cotton. Coconut husk buttons. c. 1954.

Label: **Royal Palm Tampa, Fla.** Yellow with green and brown vignettes of sporting events. Rayon. White plastic buttons.

Label: **Surf 'n Sand Made In Hawaii for Andrade Resort Shops** (over) **The Royal Hawaiian Hotel and Moana Surfrider Hotel On the Beach at Waikiki**. Red, black, and grey *Lurline* print on white pure silk. Coconut shell buttons, long sleeves. c. 1954. The Moana Surfrider Hotel (which opened in 1953) and The Royal Hawaiian Hotel were owned by Matson Navigation Co., owners of the luxury liner *Lurline*.

Label: **Shaheen's of Honolulu**. The *Lurline* oceanliner design in aqua and shades of brown on white pure silk. Coconut shell buttons, long sleeves. c. 1954.

Label: **Winifred Dick Honolulu**. The *Lurline* oceanliner, lei vendors, erupting volcanoes, outriggers, grass shacks, palm trees, and pineapples. Shades of blue on white pure silk. Coconut shell buttons. c. 1954.

Label: **Styled by Topcraft**. Dark blue with red sailboats design. Rayon. Oyster shell buttons. Two patch pockets.

Label: **marc daniels Made in U.S.A.** Red with blue, yellow, and white large sailboat. Rayon. Plastic buttons. contemporary shirt.

Label: **Archdale Rayon.** Dark blue with red sailboats. Rayon. Yellow plastic buttons. Two patch pockets.

Label: **Alii Lole made in Hawaii.** Gray with colored Hawaiian landscapes including Diamond Head, Waikiki Beach, red rainbow, waterfall, and blue palm trees. Rayon. Coconut shell buttons. Long sleeves. c. 1960.

Label: **Sportop Hand Washable.** Dark blue with sailboats and line drawings of a lighthouse and jumping dolphins. Rayon. Blue plastic buttons. Two patch pockets.

Label: **Hawaiian Holiday 100% Rayon Made in Korea RN14978**. Blue with multi-colored island landscape and hula girls. Rayon. Plastic buttons. 1960s.

Label: **B.S.R.** (separately) **100% cotton RN64371 Made in Turkey See reverse for care**. White with colorful yet simple tropical landscape. Cotton. c. after 1965.

Label: **Woodrow Stores of Florida**. Dark blue with four-color scenes of Florida labeled "Palm Beach", etc. Rayon. White plastic buttons.

Label: **Van Cort No Ironing 100% Polyester Dist. by F. W. Woolworth New York, N.Y. 10007 RN 14711 Made in Korea**. Blue landscape with building and boats. Polyester. Plastic buttons. c. 1965.

Label: **Paradise Found, Honolulu, Hawaii**.
Light blue and green with palm trees and hula
girls. Rayon. Coconut husk buttons. c. 1970.

Label: **Sun Country**. Blue with colorful
island scene. Rayon. Plastic buttons.

Fish Designs

Label: **Royal Hawaiian Honolulu**. Pink and red underwater scene with scuba divers, coral, and fish. Rayon. Coconut husk buttons. c. 1940.

Label: **Palm Breeze Togs Hawaii**. Colorful fish in shaded light brown water. Rayon. Coconut shell buttons. c. 1940.

Label: **Shaheen's of Honolulu**. Spear fisherman swimming in swirling water filled with fish. Five colors. Rayon. Coconut shell buttons, two patch pockets. This shirt was purchased from a man who bought it in the Pacific during the last year of World War II. He never wore it. c. 1945.

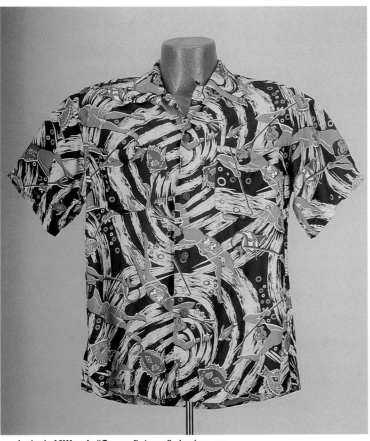

Label: **Kiilani**. "Spearfishers" design on dark blue background. Rayon. Coconut buttons. Special shirt. 1945.

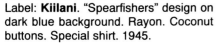

Labels: **McGregor T.M. Washable Made in U.S.A.** (separately) **Kamaaina Authentics**. Brown with multi-colored vignettes and fish design. Cotton. Brown plastic buttons. c. 1945.

Label: **Kamehameha**. Green with light blue fish and red coral. Rayon. Coconut shell buttons. A favorite of the owner because of the great colors and design. c. 1950.

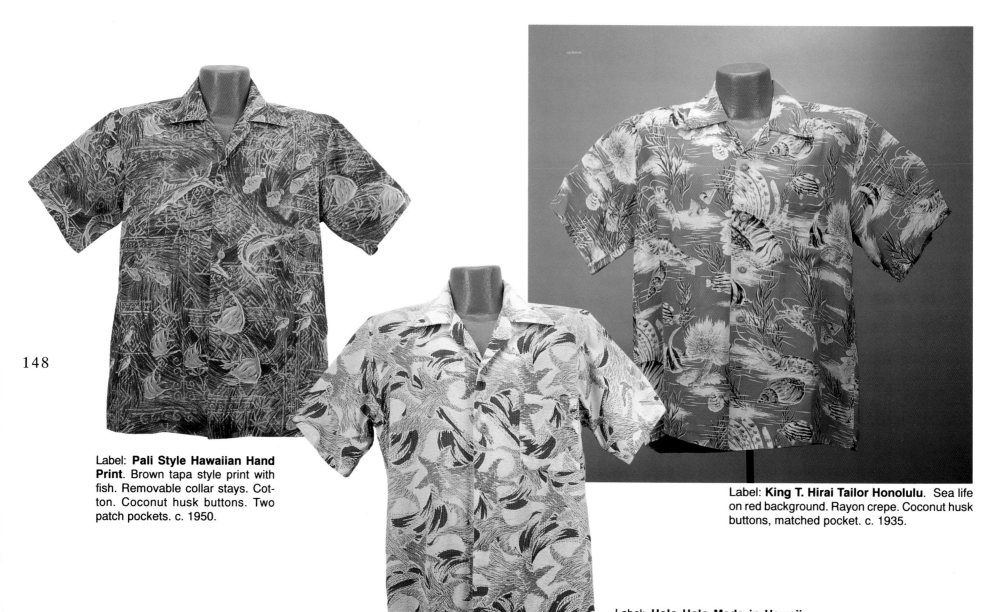

148

Label: **Pali Style Hawaiian Hand
Print**. Brown tapa style print with
fish. Removable collar stays. Cotton. Coconut husk buttons. Two
patch pockets. c. 1950.

Label: **King T. Hirai Tailor Honolulu**. Sea life
on red background. Rayon crepe. Coconut husk
buttons, matched pocket. c. 1935.

Label: **Holo Holo Made in Hawaii**.
White with star fish and fishing net
design. Cotton seersucker. Coconut
husk buttons.

Label: **Surfriders Sportswear Manufacturers Made in Honolulu Hawaii**. Both shirts with fish design, one in brown with long sleeves and the other in red with black, yellow and white with short sleeves. Cotton. Molded plastic buttons with Asian writing. Two patch pockets. c. 1955.

Label: **Iolani Made in Hawaii**. Great fish design on green background. Rayon crepe. Coconut husk buttons. c. 1955.

149

Fish salt and pepper shakers.

150

Label: **alfred Shaheen Honolulu**. Brown fish design. Cotton. Molded plastic buttons with Asian writing. c. 1955.

Label: **Shaheen's of Honolulu Made in Hawaii** (over) **Distinctive Sportswear for Discriminating People**. Brown and black fan coral with kihi kihi fish. Cotton. Coconut shell buttons. c. 1955.

Label: **Shaheen's of Honolulu Made in Hawaii** (over) **Distinctive Sportswear for Discriminating People**. Brown with yellow fish design. Cotton. Molded buttons in basket-weave design. c. 1955.

Label: **Shaheen's of Honolulu Made in Hawaii** (over) **Distinctive Sportswear for Discriminating People**. Selvage printed: **Copyright 1958 by Alfred Shaheen Ltd. "Undersea Tapa" Handprinted - Waikiki, Hawaii**. Dark shaded red with white fish and sea horses. Cotton. Plastic molded buttons with Asian writing. 1958. *See Alfred Shaheen label for selvage inscription.*

Label: **Malihini Made in Hawaii**. Light purple with spear fishermen printed on right chest. Cotton. Molded plastic buttons with Asian writing. c. 1960.

Label: **Made in Honolulu**. Red with a diving swimmer and fish. Cotton. Coconut shell buttons.

Label: None. Multi-colored fish design on yellow background. Cotton. Yellow plastic buttons.

Label: None. Wine red with kihi kihi fish and grid background design. Cotton. Coconut shell buttons.

Label: **Arrow Made in U.S.A.** Washable Rayon. Dark blue with white fish design. Rayon. White plastic buttons. Two flap pockets.

152

Label: **Styled by Topcraft**. White with swordfish design. Rayon. Oyster shell buttons. Two patch pockets.

Label: **Kennington**. (separately) **100% Rayon RN**. green with orange, yellow, and pink fish. Rayon. Plastic buttons. c. 1975.

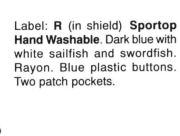

Label: **R** (in shield) **Sportop Hand Washable**. Dark blue with white sailfish and swordfish. Rayon. Blue plastic buttons. Two patch pockets.

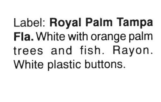

Label: **Royal Palm Tampa Fla.** White with orange palm trees and fish. Rayon. White plastic buttons.

153

Label: **Jayson Made in U.S.A.-T.M. Washable**. Dark blue with red sail boat and white dotted sailfish. Rayon. Oyster shell buttons. Two patch pockets.

Label: (blue) **Driftwood Sportswear Buttnick Mfg. Co. Seattle**. (separately) Union Made. Wine red background with colorful fish and coral design. Rayon. Yellow plastic buttons, long sleeves.

Tapa Cloth Designs

Label: **Made in Hawaii for Ross Sutherland Honolulu** (and separately) **Pure Silk**. Brown with sections of various torn tapa cloth design. Silk. Braided buttons of the same fabric. Long sleeves. c. 1940-60.

Label: **Made in Hawaii for Ross Sutherland Honolulu**. Brown abstracted floral design with a strong tapa influence. Cotton, double stitched. Coconut shell buttons, and two patch pockets. c. 1940-60.

Label: **Paradise Hawaii Made in Honolulu**. Green block print design. Cotton. Molded plastic buttons with Asian writing. c. 1960.

Label: **Duke Champion Kahanamoku Made by Cisco**. Brown with yellow, blue and orange patterned stripes. Rayon. Oyster shell buttons. c. 1948.

154

Label: **Made in Hawaii 100% cotton RN 20942**. Blue tapa design with green cape-shaped areas containing water scenes with figures. Cotton. Coconut husk buttons.

Label: (plain white) **Paradise Sportswear Made in Hawaii**. This brown print features tapa beaters and the leaves and fruit of the 'ulu (breadfruit). Cotton, double stitched. Coconut shell buttons. c. 1948-1950.

155

Label: (red) **The Kahala Made in Honolulu for The Liberty House**. Tapa vertical print in shades of blue on white. Rayon. Coconut husk buttons. This may be the print known as "aloha tapa". c. 1950.

Label: (brown with palm tree) **Paradise Sportswear Made in Hawaii**. Brown tapa beaters and breadfruit with leaves. Cotton, double stitched. Coconut shell buttons. c. 1948-1950.

156

Label: (red) **The Kahala Made in Honolulu**. Selvage printed: **Kahala Hand Screened Prints - Designed and Created in Honolulu -Molokai-**. Stylized tapa print in red, black, and silver on yellow background. Silk. Coconut shell buttons. c. 1950. *See the selvage with Kahala labels*. This print was introduced in 1949 as a "modified tapa pattern". It came in six different colors on washable silk and the short sleeve version sold for $12.50 (See *Paradise of the Pacific*, September 1949, Hawaiiana supplement, p. 3.)

Label: **Royal Hawaiian Made and styled in Hawaii**. 5-color shaded blue and yellow pattern in squares. Crepe Rayon. Coconut husk buttons. c. 1951.

Label: **Kilohana Made in Hawaii**. Brown tapa design with green floral groups. Cotton. Coconut shell buttons. c. 1954.

Label: **Malihini Made in Hawaii**. Red tapa design with blue bamboo leaves. Cotton. Coconut shell buttons. c. 1955.

Label: **Shaheen's of Honolulu** (over) **Distinctive Sportswear for Discriminating People Made in Hawaii**. Black and orange geometric tapa patterns on crackled background. Cotton. Coconut shell buttons. c. 1955.

Label: **Malihini Hale at Waikiki**. Red, black and gray tapa design. Cotton. Coconut shell buttons. c. 1955.

157

Label: **Samuel R. Kramer Fine Men's Wear Honolulu T.H. Long Beach, Calif.** This stunning shirt reproduces traditional tapa designs overlaid with the Royal Hawaiian Crest. The names of Hawaiian royalty are worked into the borders of each square of tapa: Kamehameha, Kalakaua, Liholiho, and Liliuokalani. Brown and rust on yellow. Rayon. Plastic buttons. c. 1955.

Label: **Malihini Made in Hawaii**. Dark blue and red tapa design. Cotton. Coconut shell buttons. c. 1955.

Label: **An Original Hawaiian Togs**. Made in Hawaii. Red, black, gray and white geometric pattern in diamonds design. Rayon. Coconut shell buttons. c. 1955.

Label: **An Original Hawaiian Togs Made in Hawaii**. Brown tapa geometric design. Cotton. Coconut shell buttons. c. 1955.

Label: **Shaheen's of Honolulu** (over) **Distinctive Sportswear for Discriminating People Made in Hawaii**. Brown and black tapa design. Cotton. Coconut shell buttons. c. 1955-60.

Label: **Reef Made in Hawaii**. Red tapa design overlaid with Primo beer insignia, lettering "The Happy Note in Island Refreshment," and figure with ukulele. Coconut husk buttons. c. 1957-64.

Label: (red italics) **Kamehameha made and styled in Hawaii**. Blue tapa design. Cotton. Coconut husk buttons. c. 1960.

Label: **Hoaloha Made and Styled in Hawaii**. Red tapa design with yellow and white pattern. Cotton. Coconut husk buttons. c. 1960.

Label: None. Selvage printed: **"Pohuehue Tapa" R Screen Printed at Makaha, Hawaii for Kamehameha by Hawaiian Textiles VHY**. Blue plaids and tapa design. Cotton. Metal clad molded buttons of King Kamehameha statue and labeled "Kamehameha." c. 1962. *See the selvage with Hawaiian Textiles label.*

Label: **Leslie's at Waikiki Honolulu**. Brown vertical tapa print. Cotton. Coconut shell buttons. c. 1964.

Label: **Created in Hawaii for Island Casuals International Market Place Waikiki**. Brown tapa and floral design. Cotton. Metal buttons with Asian writing. c. 1964.

160

Label: **Created in Hawaii for Diamond Head Sportswear International Market Place Waikiki**. Gray tapa design. Cotton. Light coconut buttons. c. 1964.

Label: **Surfriders Sportswear Manufacturers Made in Honolulu Hawaii**. Brown and blue tapa design with overlaid yellow flowers. Cotton. Coconut shell buttons.

Label: **Made in Hawaii for Hawaiian Sport Shop Ft. Lauderdale, Surfside, Florida**. Brown tapa design with sea shells. Cotton. Molded plastic buttons with the Hawaiian royal crest and lettering "Aloha - Hawaii."

Label: **Made in Hawaii**. Multi-colored floral and tapa design. Cotton. Coconut husk buttons.

Label: **Paradise Hawaii Made in Honolulu**.
Green tapa design. Cotton. Molded silver
plastic buttons with Asian writing. c. 1960.

Label: **Made in Hawaii**. Turquoise
with scattered tapa designs. Cotton.
Gray plastic buttons.

Label: **Made in Hawaii for Hawaiian Sport
Shop Inc. Ft. Lauderdale, Bay Harbor Is-
land, Florida**. Green tapa design with fish.
Cotton. Coconut shell buttons.

Border Prints

Label: **Watumull's Honolulu, Hawaii**. Woman's face and flowers in red and green vertical design on a white background. Rayon. White buttons. Long sleeves, never been worn. c. 1945.

Label: **Duke Champion Kahanamoku An Hawaiian Original**. Dark blue with multi-colored large floral and pineapple design border print. Rayon. Oyster shell buttons. c. 1940.

162

Label: **Kiilani Made in Honolulu**. Floral vertical print in seven colors on red background. Rayon. Coconut shell buttons. c. 1945.

Label: **Duke Champion Kahanamoku An Hawaiian Original**. Dark blue background with four-color floral border print. Rayon. Oyster shell buttons. c. 1940.

Label: (large) **Duke Champion Kahanamoku Made by Cisco**. Dark blue background with a 5-color floral design border print. Rayon. Oyster shell buttons. c. 1948.

Label: **Duke Champion Kahanamoku Made by Cisco Unconditionally Washable**. Multi-color border print with Navy blue background and scene of Diamond Head viewed from inside a grove of graceful coconut palms. Rayon. Oyster shell buttons, two patch pockets. c. 1948. This is the same shirt design as the shirt worn by Montgomery Clift in the death scene of the 1954 movie *From Here To Eternity*.

164

Label: None. Dark red with yellow and black floral border print. Particularly heavy weight Rayon. Oyster shell buttons. Long sleeves.

Label: Missing. Blue palm trees border print on white background. Rayon. Oyster shell buttons.

165

Label: **royal palm in a sport wear ellallinson fabric of Rayon Reg. U.S. Pat. Off. Styled and Made in Miami**. Dark blue background with huge palm tree border print. Rayon. Oyster shell buttons. Two waist patch pockets.

Label: (large rectangle) **Duke Champion Kahanamoku Made By Cisco**. Unconditionally Washable. Gray palm trees border print on red background. Rayon. Oyster shell buttons. c. 1948.

166

Label: **Kiilani Made in Honolulu**. Blue background with detailed print of native Hawaiians, very rare design. Rayon. Coconut shell buttons. Special shirt. c. 1945.

Label: **Duke Champion Kahanamoku Made by Cisco Unconditionally Washable Rayon**. Dark brown with four-color border print in rows of palm trees, sail boats, fish, and pineapples and huts. Rayon. Oyster shell buttons. c. 1948.

Label: Missing. Dark blue with light blue, gray and white patterned squares and solid placket. Rayon. Oyster shell buttons.

Label: (green) **Kamehameha made and styled in Hawaii**. Red tapa design. Cotton. Coconut shell buttons. c. 1950.

Label: (green) **Kamehameha Made and Styled in Hawaii**. Five color vertical Niu (coconut palm loaded with fruit) design on red background. Rayon. Coconut husk buttons. c. 1950.

Label: (large rectangle) **Duke Champion Kahanamoku Made by Cisco Unconditionally Washable**. Brown and aqua geometric and rosette pattern with solid brown front placket. Rayon. Oyster shell buttons. Two patch pockets. c. 1948.

Label: (blue) **Made in Hawaii**. Five color Niu (coconut palm loaded with fruit) on a blue background. Rayon. Coconut husk buttons. c. 1950.

Label: (green) **Kamehameha Made and Styled in Hawaii** (separately) hanging tag: **Paradise Print Hand Washable**. Philodendron monstera vertical print in five colors on blue background. Rayon. Coconut shell buttons. This shirt has never been worn. c. 1950.

168

Label: **alfred Shaheen Honolulu**. Shaded blue floral border design. Cotton. Molded plastic buttons with Asian writing. c. 1955-60.

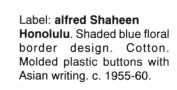

Label: **alfred Shaheen Honolulu**. Gray and brown border print with sailboats and fish. Cotton. Molded plastic buttons with Asian writing. c. 1955-60.

Label: (green) **Kamehameha Made and Styled in Hawaii For Watumull's**. Vertical floral print in five colors on black background. Rayon. Coconut shell buttons. A phenomenal shirt! c. 1950.

Label: **Styled by Aloha Tailor Wahiawa**. Botanical vertical print in four colors on red background. Rayon. Coconut husk buttons. c. 1953. Wahiawa sits astride the saddle between the Koolau and Waianae mountain ranges, a prime sugar cane and pineapple growing region. Within two miles of Wahiawa is the sprawling Army base known as Schofield Barracks, the setting of the James Jones novel *From Here to Eternity* which was made into a popular Hollywood movie in 1954.

169

Label: **Tropical Prints by McCoy Washable**. Brown with light green and yellow flowers. Rayon. Oyster shell buttons. Two patch pockets.

Bathrobe and fabric belt. Label: **Made by Shaheen's of Honolulu** (over) **Distinctive Sportswear for Discriminating People Made in Hawaii**. Maroon background with green and yellow border print of leaves and geometric design. Rayon. c. 1950-55.

Label: **Made in Hawaii for Ross Sutherland Honolulu**. Under the sea vertical print in four colors on red background. Rayon. Coconut shell buttons. c. 1940-60.

Left Label: **Wolf Brothers Tampa Florida.** Red with white and turquoise vertical design. Rayon. Oyster shell buttons. Two patch pockets and long sleeves.

Below Label: **The Liberty House Honolulu Waikiki**. Sea shell border print in three colors on a red background. Rayon. Coconut shell buttons. This shirt has never been worn.

Label: **An Original Hawaiian Togs Made in Hawaii 100% Cotton**. Light blue floral border print. Cotton. Metal buttons. c. 1960.

Label: (blue) **An Original "Poi Pounder Tog" Hawaiian Togs - Honolulu**. Red background with U.S. military personnel and insignia, heavily labeled map of Oahu, 25th Division locations in Korea, 14th locations in Korea '51-'53. This must be a custom print for a military reunion. Rayon crepe. Coconut husk buttons. c. 1960.

Label: (red italics) **Kamehameha made and styled in Hawaii**. Black and brown floral border print. Cotton. Coconut husk buttons. c. 1960.

Label: None. Red with white vertical symmetrical design. Cotton. Coconut shell buttons.

Right Label: **Resort Line Hawaii**. Blue border print with red bird of paradise and palm leaves. Polyester. Plastic buttons, Very contemporary. c. 1970.

Below Label: **Mark Twain Reg. U.S. Pst. Off. Pleisure Shirt**. Dark blue background with colorful vertical floral print. Rayon. White buttons. Long sleeves.

172

Above Label: **Pomaré Tahiti Honolulu Hawaii RN 37145**. Bright red and pink vertical orchid design. Polyester. Pink plastic buttons. c. 1970. Kind of a disco Hawaiian shirt, if there ever were such an animal.

Label: None. Pullover style of red with white flowers. Cotton. Plastic buttons. 1970s.

173

Label: (red) **Island Fashions Made in U.S.A.** Horizontal border print of ocean waves, sailboat, palm trees and flowers on a dark rose background with brown and blue stripes and a solid light pink bottom. Cotton. White plastic buttons. c. 1980.

Photo Designs

Pair of kissing bobbing head figures.

Label: **Palm Breeze Togs Hawaii**. Postcard views featuring eruptions of the volcano Kilauea in multi-colors on gray background. Rayon crepe. Coconut shell buttons, matching pocket and front plackets. This is a magnificent shirt! c. 1940.

Label: **Made in Hawaii for Ross Sutherland Honolulu**. Blue Hawaiian themes on an Oriental background. Silk. Coconut shell buttons, matched pocket. c. 1940-60.

Label: **Palm Breeze Togs Hawaii**. Yellow with woodblock prints of Asian landscapes in nine colors on white. Silk. Coconut shell buttons, matched pocket and front plackets. c. 1940.

175

176

Label: **Royal Hawaiian Quality Garments Made in Honolulu**. Red with Japanese folding screen landscapes. Multi-colors on white pure silk. Coconut husk buttons, matching pocket and front plackets. c. 1955.

Label: **Kuu-Ipo Made in Hawaii**. Multi-colored
photographic picture shirt with scenes from
Hawaii. Rayon. Coconut husk buttons. c.1951.

Buttons

Original buttons on aloha shirts have helped to tell the story of the shirt style's development. From early colored plastics and oyster shell, to coconut husk and coconut shell, to stamped metal and back to plastics again, analysis of their different types is another "exercise in madness" that a few dedicated enthusiasts enjoy.

Besides a Kodak store in Honolulu selling coconut buttons in 1935 (see the text section for the 1930s), another anecdote on the subject of buttons has been gleaned:

178

Dorothy Shimabukuro... works late each evening at her modest Emerson Street home making intricate Chinese buttons for Hawaii's garment industry. Daytime she gets her materials ready.

She has turned out as many as 600 in a night — 10,000 in a month.

And her feat is made all the more remarkable by the fact that Mrs. Shimabukuro is blind. She is one of 24 sightless men and women for whom work is subcontracted through clothing manufacturers by the State Home Industry Program in the Department of Social Services

Started [in 1957]...More than 50 per cent of the clothing manufacturers have participated in the program since its inception...

The manufacturers turn over bias material to [a woman] in the afternoon for delivery to the button-makers. She picks up the finished product by 8 o'clock the next morning.

The rigid schedule is necessary... because the strips of bias cannot be obtained until the garment is cut. And there are relatively few steps between material on the cutting table and the nearly completed... [garment] ready for finishing touches. ("Blind Woman is Expert Button Maker," *Honolulu Advertiser*, November 13, 1961, Section B, p. 9.)

Oyster shell, wide rim

Oyster shell, medium rim

Oyster shell, narrow rim

Colored plastics

Asian writing

Head with helmet

Man's head & "Hawaii"

Royal shield

Silver metal & plastic King Kamehameha

Gold metal & plastic King Kamehameha

Metal flower head

Metal basket weave

Stamped flat leather

Domed plastic, looks like leather

Plastic, looks like bamboo

Braided fabric, "Chinese style"

Braided fabric, "Chinese style"

Coconut shell, flat

Coconut shell, indented

Coconut husk

Manufacturers and Retail Labels

Aloha shirts and Hawaiian sportswear have hundreds of different manufacturer's and retailer's labels representing the many firms competing in the marketplace. This compilation is not at all complete (can it ever be?) but it probably represents most of the well-known and more prolific Hawaiian companies, associated with aloha shirts, operating primarily in the 1935 to 1965 period. Some of these labels come from before and some from after that central period, as popular styles gradually evolve and are repeated. This list is presented only as a general guide.

The labelling of shirts has a long history among Hawaiian shirt manufacturers. The first garment manufacturing factory in Hawaii, the Hawaiian Clothing Manufacturing Company, Ltd, in 1922, included a sketch of its trademark in the first advertisement which the firm placed. (*Polk-Husted Directory*, 1922, p. 355.)

Since the late 1930s, Hawaiian aloha shirt manufacturers have either sold under the label of the company or under the label of a brand name. Branfleet used the Kahala brand label. Firms in Hawaii have marketed their shirts under a variety of labeling arrangements, including using the label of the garment manufacturer; the label of the retailer; two separate labels in the shirt, one for the retailer and one for the manufacturer; a joint label for the retailer and the manufacturer; or a label that reads "Made in Hawaii." In addition, the label of a fiber or fabric is sometimes used.

Where the label of a retailer is used, it may have the name of the retail firm on it, or it may have a brand name of the retailer. An example of a joint label may be found in some of the shirts sold by McInerny of Honolulu, such as those of Kahala Sportswear, Ltd. A label which has the manufacturer and the brand name is "Duke Kahanamoku Made in Hawaii by Kahala." Some use only the name of the manufacturer, such as "Diane's" or "Lauhala Sportswear." Sometimes, when a manufacturer sells under a brand name or names, the company name is smaller and the brand name is larger. When the company's name only is used on a label, the advertising gives the buyer and the consumer a single name to remember.

Some shirt labels have a sketch in addition to the name of the company or the brand name, such as a grass hut, palm tree, bamboo, etc.

Some labels are registered. When shirts are sold by a manufacturer, the manufacturer is required to secure from the United States Federal Trade Commission a registration number (RN number) so that the products may be traced or identified. The manufacturer is responsible for the quality as advertised.

179

The labels of Hawaiian garment manufacturers are usually designed in Hawaii and are often manufactured in Japan. (Fundaburk, Vol. 3, p. 199-205.)

Alfred Shaheen Honolulu
See Shaheen's of Honolulu and Surf 'n Sand. Alfred Shaheen started printing fabrics in 1947 at 1687 Kalauokalani Way, Honolulu. In 1952, the fabric printing and aloha shirt production were under the name Surf 'n Sand Hand Prints Ltd. In 1956, Alfred Shaheen Ltd. was organized and a new fabric printing plant was built on Kalakaua Avenue, Honolulu. By 1964, Alfred Shaheen Stores, Ltd. was organized to sell men's sportswear and shops were opened at the Ala Moana Center, the Hilton Hawaiian Village, and 2252 Kalakaua Avenue Waikiki in Honolulu, and at 284 Kamehameha Avenue in Hilo.

Alii Lole Made in Hawaii
Alii Distributors, Inc., founded in 1955 at 1044 Bethel Street, Honolulu, is listed as a shirt manufacturer. The words *Alii Lole* mean "royal clothing."

Aloha Tailor Wahiawa
A manufacturer of shirts & clothing at 38 Walikina Drive, Wahiawa, Aloha Tailor, Ltd. was founded in 1937 by George Takato and was listed from 1952 as a sportswear maker.

Aloha Kanaka Original by Artvogue

Alpine Sportswear Inc. Dallas

Andrade Resort Shops
Retail store in Honolulu at the Men's shop at the Royal Hawaiian Hotel from before the 1930s. In 1964, Andrade & Co, Ltd. also had the Women's Apparel Shop at the Royal Hawaiian Hotel and five other locations in Honolulu selling men's sportswear at Ala Moana Center, Downtown Honolulu 1027 Fort Street, Moana-Surfrider Hotel lobby, Avenue shop 2384 Kalakaua Avenue, and the Resort shop at Halekulani Hotel.

Archdale

Arrow Made in U. S. A.

Ashfield by Duke of Hollywood Ca. Made in California

Bali Specially made for Navy Exchange Guam M.I.

Balsam

B. S. R. Made in Turkey

Branfleet Sportswear
See Kahala and text. Founded in 1936 by George Brangier and Nathaniel Norfleet as a major shirt maker and sales organization, especially to the U.S. mainland and listed until 1949. Became Kahala Sportswear, Ltd. in 1951. Branfleet did not label shirts under the Branfleet name, but used the Kahala label and had the Duke Kahanamoku Champion shirts from 1936 to about 1943 when Cisco began selling this line. In 1961, Branfleet again had the Duke line.
Duke Kahanamoku was an Olympic champion swimmer and sheriff of Honolulu.

Burma Gold Handprints
See Sears, Roebuck & Company. Hand Prints Made & Styled in Hawaii Exclusively for Sears.

Campus

Capistrano reg'd by Wismar Made in California

catchit

Central Pacific Importers of Hawaii Made in Japan

Cisco
See Branfleet and Duke Kahanamoku. Presumably a New York company, possibly connected with Branfleet, which sold the Duke Kahanamoku Champion shirts between about 1943 and 1960.

Del Mar Sportswear Made in California

Diamond Head Sportswear, International Market Place, Waikiki Sold sportswear retail in 1964.

Diane Honolulu
Diane's Inc. was founded in 1943 by Diane Uchimura to manufacture women's sportswear.

Don Juan of California Made in California

Dr. Beach Made in U.S.A. of imported fabric

Driftwood Sportswear, Buttnick Mfg. Co. Seattle

Duke Kahanamoku
See Branfleet and Cisco. A line of Branfleet Sportswear from about 1936 to 1943 and again in 1961. Between 1943 and 1960, the Duke Champion line was sold by Cisco.

Flying Fish Made in Japan

Golden Gate Made in California

Grosdale Sportswear

Guymont

Hale Hawaii Made in Hawaii
Hale Hawaii, Ltd. was first listed in 1951 at 1706 N. King Street, Honolulu, and was not listed after 1962. The words *Hale Hawaii* mean "Hawaiian house."

Hale-Niu Honolulu
A 1946 advertisement was for Hale-Niu Sportswear. Hale-Niu Sportswear, Inc. was listed from 1950, selling retail in 1964 in Honolulu, and selling bowling shirts in 1965. The term *Hale Niu* means "house of coconut."

181

Hana-Maui Shop Custom Apparel

harper Sportswear

182

Hauoli Kamaaina Authentic Hawaiian Prints Made in California

Hawaii Blues Made in Korea

Hawaii Clothing Manufacturing Co.
Founded in 1922 to manufacture 'Men's, Ladies' and Children's Wearing Apparel' and advertised until 1930. In 1932, the company's name was changed to Sailor Moku Products, Ltd. as their primary product was denim trousers by that name.

Hawaiian Casuals by Stan Hicks Made in Honolulu
Stanley T. Hicks was president. Listed as Hawaiian Casuals from 1951 to 1957 and as Hawaiian Casuals, Ltd. from 1958 to 1964. In 1960, Hawaiian Casuals Maui Branch is listed.

Hawaiian Holiday Made in Korea

Hawaiian Print Made in California Washable

Hawaiian Prints
See Washington Shirt Co. label.

Hawaiian Sport Shop, Inc. Ft. Lauderdale and Bay Harbor Island, Florida Made in Hawaii

Hawaiian Surf
See Pacific Sportswear.

Hawaiian Textiles Created in Hawaii
From 1899 to about 1956, Von Hamm-Young & Co was a dry goods store in Honolulu. In 1957, they began to print plain fabrics for shirt manufacturers as Hawaiian Textiles Company.

Hawaiian Togs Made in Hawaii
Hawaiian Togs, Ltd., founded in 1947 at 835 Keeaumoku Street to manufacture sportswear.

Hawaiiana Modes Designed in Hawaii
Listed 1963-64.

Hilo Hattie Made in Hawaii
Hilo Hattie was a popular Hawaiian singer and entertainer in the 1940s.

T. Hirai Tailor & Sportswear
See King label. Listed 1952 to 1962 as a clothing manufacturer and in 1964 as retail sportswear shop at 2716 S. King St. in Honolulu.

Hoaloha Made and styled in Hawaii
See Sears, Roebuck. Label used by Sears, Roebuck and Company on some Hawaiian apparel it advertised in 1958 to 1960. The word *Hoaloha* means "friend."

Holo-Holo Made in Hawaii
Holo Holo Apparel Manufacturing Co. was founded 1946 at 1428 E. Makaloa Street, Honolulu, to manufacture sportswear. The term *Holo-Holo* means "to go out for pleasure."

Honolulu Garment Mfg, Co.
See Kihi Kihi label. Listed 1947 to 1956 as clothing manufacturer.

Hookano Brand Made in Hawaii
Hookano Sportswear was founded in 1946 at 922 Austin Lane, Honolulu. The word *Hookano* means "proud."

Hoomaha Made and Styled in Hawaii
The word *Hoomaha* means "vacation."

Imperial

Iolani Made in Hawaii
Iolani Sportswear, Ltd. was founded by Keiji Kawakami in 1953 as a clothing manufacturer. A branch operated at 1218 Kona Street, Hanapee, Kauai. The word *Iolani* is the name of the Palace in Honolulu, in front of which stands the statue of Kamehameha as shown on most of the labels.

Island Casuals, International Market Place, Waikiki
Sold sportswear retail in 1964.

Island Fashions

Jantzen Made in U.S.A.
*See Kona * Kai and Nani Sportswear, Ltd.*
Jantzen Sportswear acquired Nani Sportswear, Ltd. in 1950 and retained the name until it was liquidated in 1964.

Jayson Made in U. S. A.

The Kahala Made in Honolulu
See Branfleet. The Kahala Hand Screened Prints label was used by Branfleet Sportswear. In 1951, Branfleet changed its name to Kahala Sportswear, Ltd. at 1329 Kamaile Street, Honolulu. In 1961, Kahala Sportswear, Ltd. started a new line of Duke Kahanamoku shirts after a period from about 1943 to 1960 when the Duke line was sold by Cisco.

Kahana Manufacturing Co. Honolulu
Founded in 1944 at 1143 Young Street to manufacture women's sportswear.

Kaikamahine Honolulu
Listed from 1953 to 1955 as a clothing manufacturer. One shirt has a statehood print, so maybe they were in business in 1959. The word *Kaikamahine* means "girl."

Ka-lae Hawaii

Kalakaua Made in Hawaii
The word *Kalakaua* is the name of the last Hawaiian King and the man responsible for saving traditional Hawaiian culture from oblivion, King David Kalakaua.

Kamaaina Authentics
See McGregor label

Kamehameha Made and Styled in Hawaii
Kamehameha Garment Co., Ltd. was founded in 1936 by Herbert V. Briner at 800-B South Beretania Street, Honolulu, to make sportswear and sell it primarily to overseas markets. In 1954, a plant was also operated at 713 Sheridan Street, Hilo. The Eugene Savage mural designs were printed on fabric for shirts by this company. The word *Kamehameha* comes from King Kamehameha, the conqueror of the Islands and first King of all the Hawaiian islands.

Kealoha of Hawaii Hand Painted Garment
See Nani.

Kennington

Kihi Kihi Made in Hawaii
Honolulu Garment Mfg. Co.
See Honolulu Garment Mfg. Co. Kihi Kihi is listed in 1937 and 1938 as a manufacturer of wearing apparel, wholesale only. Also, a shirt with a 50th state design (c. 1959) has a label "Kihi Kihi Sportswear Made in Hawaii." The word *Kihi-Kihi* is the Hawaiian name of the Moorish Idol fish.

Kiilani Made in Honolulu

Kilohana Made in Hawaii
Listed in 1953-1954 as a manufacturer of Hawaiian sportswear. The word *Kilohana* means "the best" and refers to the decorated tapa outer sheet of bed coverings.

King, T. Hirai Tailor, Honolulu
See T. Hirai Tailor.

King-Smith
See text. King-Smith dry goods store was at 36 N. King Street near Smith in Honolulu in the 1930s and was listed in 1936 as a clothing manufacturer. King-Smith owner Ellery Chun applied for a trade mark for "Aloha" sportswear in 1936 and registered the label "Aloha" in 1937. A 1939 ad reads "creator of `Aloha' shirts and `Waikiki' Fashions." Chun continued to run the business until 1950.

Kona Kai made in Hawaii for Sears
See Sears, Roebuck and Company.

Kona * Kai Hawaiian Casuals
Made in U.S.A. by jantzen
See Hawaiian Casuals and Jantzen.

Samuel R. Kramer Fine Men's Wear
Honolulu, T.H. Long Beach, Calif.

Kramer's Honolulu
Kramer's retail shop was at 1102 Fort Street, Honolulu, in 1964.

Styled by Kuhio Sportswear
Honolulu Hawaii
Kuhio Sportswear, Ltd. was listed in 1952.

184

Kulani Beach Tropical Sportswear

Kuonakakai Authentic Hawaiian Original
See National Shirt Shops, c. 1948.
Kuonakakai is the name of the largest town on the island of Molokai.

Kuu-Ipo Made in Hawaii
The words *Kuu-Ipo* mean "My sweetheart."

Lauhala Made in Hawaii
Lauhala Sportswear, Inc. was founded in 1943 to manufacture sportswear with an address at 1722 Kalakaua Avenue and Hanapepe, Kauai (possibly as a branch in 1965). Lauhala Sales Co. is mentioned in a 1948 Sears, Roebuck and Company advertisement, is in the 1949 city directory as manufacturers and wholesalers of Hawaiian sportswear, and is listed from 1952 to 1964. The word *Lauhala* means the pandanus leaf as used in plaiting.

Lehua Hilo, Hawaii
The word *Lehua* is the name of the flower of the ohia tree.

Lei-O-Hawaii Sportswear
Listed from 1960 as a manufacturer of wearing apparel.

Leisure Club Sportogs

Leslie's at Waikiki Honolulu
Retail sportswear shop at 2236 Kalakaua Ave. in 1964.

The Liberty House Honolulu Waikiki
The Liberty House retail store in Honolulu began about 1850. A 1929 newspaper advertisement for The Liberty House resort fashions read, "...for 79 years we have been importing." In 1964, four locations in Hawaii were at: Downtown 1032 Fort Street, 4211 Waialea Avenue, and 2314 Kalakaua Avenue in Honolulu, and at 573 Kailau Road, Kailua (Kona).

Macy's Men's Store Sportswear Made in California
Macy's main department store is on 5th Avenue in New York City with branches in other cities.

Made in California

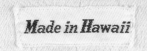

Made in Hawaii
A major effort to use the "Made in Hawaii" label on clothing was initiated in 1950.

185

Made in Honolulu

Maile Made in Japan

Malihini Made in Hawaii
Malihini Sportswear, Inc. was founded in 1946 at 746 Ilaniwai Street in Honolulu. It was listed from 1952 as a clothing manufacturer. In 1964, the Malihini Shop for women's clothes was at the Moanalua Shopping Center. The word *Malihini* means "newcomer" or "tourist."

Malihini Hale at Waikiki
The retail shop Malihini Hale sold sportswear at 2232 Kalakaua Ave. in Honolulu in 1964. The label shown resembles the Hale Hawaii label design with a grass hut and palm tree.

Manhattan

marc daniels Made in U.S.A.

Mark Twain Pleisure Shirt

Marlboro Sportswear

Marshall Field & Company The Store for Men Made in Honolulu
See Marshall Field & Company's main department store is on Michigan Avenue in Chicago with branches in other cities.

McGregor Made in U.S.A. Kamaaina Authentics

McInerny's Quality Since 1850 Honolulu
M. McInerny, Ltd. retail store began in Honolulu in 1850 and advertised aloha shirts continuously through the period under discussion. In 1964 there were six retail shops at: the Ala Moana Center, 102 S. King Street, Kaimuki Store 3650 Waialea Avenue, Reef Hotel Shop 2169 Kalia Road, Waikiki Biltmore Hotel shop 2424 Kalakaua Avenue, and Waikiki Store 2269 Kalakaua Avenue.

Mildred's of Hawaii
Founded in 1952 by Mildred Dohi.

Miracle Mohawk Sportswear

Musa-Shiya the Shirtmaker Honolulu Hawaii
See text. A dry goods store (name not known) in Honolulu was founded by Chotaro Miyamoto before 1915 (perhaps as early as 1890). It was run after 1915 by his son Kiochiro. In the 1920s, Kiochiro began making shirts (presumably from the store) in a business called Musa-Shiya The Shirtmaker. In a 1934 advertisement, the shop address is given as "My only one shop 1915 S. King Streets nearly corner Alakea Streets" and in 1935 it was advertised at 179 N. King St. In 1935, Musa-Shiya The Shirtmaker placed the first advertisement using the term 'Aloha' shirts. An address at 2164 Kalakaua Avenue is not dated. The company was not listed in 1952.

Nali'i Fashions, Ltd.
Listed from 1952 as clothing manufacturer, primarily for the tots to teens market.

Nani of Hawaii Honolulu
Founded by Betty Robertson and listed from 1949 until 1963. Acquired by Jantzen sportswear in 1950. Liquidated in 1964. The word *Nani* means "beautiful."

National Shirt Shops
See Kuonakakai. Circa 1948.

Network

Pacific Sportswear
See Hawaiian Surf. Pacific Sportswear Shop listed in Honolulu from 1947 to 1951. Pacific Sportswear Manufacturing Co. listed in Honolulu from 1951.

Pali Hawaiian Style
Founded in 1949.
The word *Pali* means "cliff." The pictures on these labels depict the famous Nuuanu Pali and Pali Road on Oahu, where Kamehameha defeated the Oahuan army in the 1700s.

Palm Breeze Togs Hawaii

Paradise Hawaii. Made in Honolulu

Paradise Found Honolulu, Hawaii

187

Paradise Sportswear Made in Hawaii
Founded in 1945. Branch in Hilo in 1964.

Pennleigh

Pennshire Sportswear for Leisure

Penney's Topflight

Pikaki Made in Hawaii
Listed as clothing manufacturer in 1963 and 1964. Pikaki Fashions retail store at 602 Queen Street, Honolulu and Hilo Shopping Center, Hilo in 1964. The word *Pikaki* is the Hawaiian term for the flower of the shrub white Arabian jasmine, a native of India.

Play Time Made in Japan

Pohaku Made in Hawaii
The word *Pohaku* means "stone."

"Poi Pounder Tog" Hawaiian Togs - Honolulu
See Hawaiian Togs. Circa after 1947.

Poinciana Sportswear

Polynesian Sportswear Made in Hawaii
Polynesian Sportswear Manufacturers listed as a clothing manufacturer from 1953 to 1959. Polynesian Casuals, Inc. listed from 1958.

Pomará Tahiti Honolulu, Hawaii

Pony Express Made in California

Random Wear Authentically Styled

Reef Made in Hawaii
Reef Sportswear Inc. founded in 1956 at 938 Austin Lane, Honolulu.

Resort Line Hawaii

Richman Brothers Made in California

Ross Sutherland Honolulu Made in Hawaii
Sutherland's at Waikiki retail store specializing in beach clothes mentioned in a 1940 article. An article from 1946 quotes Ross F. Sutherland of McInerny Ltd. In 1964, three Ross Sutherland retail stores selling men's wear were listed at 2200 Kalakaua Ave, Hilton Hawaiian Village, and Ilikai Hotel.

Royal Hawaiian
See Watumull's. Royal Hawaiian Manufacturing Co. was founded in 1937 by Max Lewis on Beretania St., Honolulu, opposite the Central Fire Station. This company became owned by G. J. Watumull by 1947 when it was located at 1166 Fort Street. It produced "silks and cottons for use in the making of island type clothing." By 1958 it was "atop the Watumull Store building on Fort Street." All of Royal Hawaiian's clothing production was sold at Watumull's East India Stores at that time.

royal palm...Styled and Made in Miami

Royal Palm Tampa Florida

Sailor Moku Products Ltd.
See Hawaii Clothing Manufacturing Co.

Sears Hawaii
See Burma Gold Handprints, Hoaloha (ca. 1958-1960), *Kona Kai,* and *Lauhala* (ca. 1948) as some labels used on aloha shirts and sportswear by retail chain Sears, Roebuck and Company with main office in Chicago, catalog sales nationwide, and stores in other cities. Advertisments for their store in Honoluu date from 1947.

Shaheen's of Honolulu
See Alfred Shaheen and *Surf 'n Sand.* About 1947, the George A. Shaheen Co., Ltd. changed from a custom tailor to a factory manufacturer of shirts, and in 1949 it advertised "Hawaiian Sportswear for Men, Ladies and Children" when it was known as "Shaheen's of Honolulu." When son Alfred Shaheen joined the business in 1947, the firm began to develop its own screen printing process for fabric and it became the dominant fabric printer in Hawaii through the 1950s.

Shapely by Mack

Silver of Hawaii Made in Japan
Silver & Co. is listed as a clothing manufacturer in Hawaii from 1955 until 1964.

Sportop

Sun Country

Sun Fashions of Hawaii, Ltd.
Listed as a clothing manufacturer in Honolulu from 1953.

Surf and Shore Honolulu, Hawaii

Surf 'n Sand Made in Honolulu
See Alfred Shaheen and Shaheen's of Honolulu. In 1952, Surf 'n Sand Hand Prints Ltd. was begun by Alfred Shaheen to screen print fabric and produce aloha shirts. This firm grew to dominate Hawaiian fabric production in the 1950s.

Surfriders Sportswear Manufacturers Made in Honolulu Hawaii
Surfriders Sportswear, Inc. was founded in 1940 at 2142 Kalakaua Avenue in Honolulu to manufacture ready-made and made-to-order sportswear. They had a retail outlet on Kapiolani Blvd. in 1940 and advertised "Hawaiian sportswear for the entire family" in 1954. Their listings continue into the 1960s.

Textile Company of America

189

Topcraft

Tori Richard, Ltd.
Listed designing sportswear from 1956. Started by fashion designer Janice Robinson and run by her husband Mortimer Feldman in the early 1960s when they imported European fabrics.

Trade-Wind-Fashion The Liberty House Waikiki on the Beach at Waikiki Honolulu, Hawaii

Tropical Prints by McCoy

Tropical Sport Shirt by c G c marca registrada

Tropicals

Tropicana
Tropicana Sportswear Manufacturing Inc. was founded in 1945 at 1536 Makaloa Street in Hololulu to produce sportswear.

Tropicool Sportswear

Tru-Lustre Sportswear

Union Supply Company
Founded in 1922 as a plantation uniform and shoe manufacturer, especially of "sailor-moku" denim trousers.

Van Cort Dist. by F. W. Woolworth New York, N. Y. 10007 Made in Korea.

Waikiki Kasuals Made in Hawaii
The word *Waikiki* means "spouting water" and is the name of the famous beach on Oahu in the shadow of Diamond Head cliff.

Waikiki Originals The Liberty House Waikiki on the Beach at Waikiki Honolulu, Hawaii *See Liberty House.*

Waikiki Sports Honolulu, Hawaii
Waikiki Sports retail shop at 2331 Kala-kaua Avenue in Honolulu was listed in 1964 selling men's and women's wear.

Waikikian Quality Sportswear Honolulu, Hawaii

Washington Shirt Co. Sportswear Hawaiian Prints

Watumull's Honolulu Made in Hawaii
See Royal Hawaiian Manufacturing Co.
Watumull's East India Shop on Fort Street was owned by G. J. Watumull and listed as a retail shop from the 1930s on. By 1947, Mr. Watumull owned the Royal Hawaiian Manufacturing Company to produce island type clothing for sale in his shop. By 1964 there were seven retail shops at Watumull's Downtown 1162 Fort Street, Ala Moana Center, Ilikai Hotel, Moana Surfrider Hotel, Ocean Tower Shop at Hilton Hawaiian Village, Princess Kaiulani Hotel, and Waikiki 2177 Kalakaua Avenue.

Watumull's and Leilani Made in Hawaii

Westwood Casuals Klein-Norton Co. Made in California

Winifred Dick Honolulu

Wolf Brothers Tampa Florida

Woodrow Stores of Florida

Young Aloha Honolulu

Bibliography

Blackburn, Mark. *Hawaiiana, The Best of Hawaiian*. Atglen: Schiffer Publishing, Ltd., 1996.

Brown, DeSoto [David T.]. *Hawaii Recalls, Selling Romance to America, Nostalgic Images of the Hawaiian Islands: 1910-1950*. Honolulu: Editions Limited, 1982.

Fundaburk, Emma Lila, Ph. D. *The Garment Manufacturing Industry of Hawaii*. Honolulu: Economic Research Center, University of Hawaii, 1965.

Honolulu Advertiser. 1935-1964.

Honolulu Star-Bulletin. 1932-1964.

Paradise of the Pacific.1920-1964.

Piercy, Larue W. *Hawaii This & That, Answers to Most Frequently Asked Questions*. Honolulu: Mutual Publishing, 1981.

Pukui, Mary Kawena and Samuel H. Elbert. *Hawaiian Dictionary*. Honolulu: University of Hawaii Press. 1986.

Steel, H. Thomas. *The Hawaiian Shirt Its Art and History*. New York: Abbeville Press, 1984.

Te Rangi Hiroa (Peter H. Buck). *Arts and Crafts of Hawaii*. Section V "Clothing" Special Publication 45. [Honolulu]: Bernice P. Bishop Museum , 1964.

Index